LONG DISTANCE PATHS

South-East England

Alan Castle

A & C Black · London

For Ron and Andrée

Acknowledgements

I would like to thank John Margetts and Sue Ramsey of the Long
Distance Walkers Association and Iain Liddell of the Long Distance
Paths Advisory Service for their assistance in providing information.
My gratitude, as always, goes to my wife, Beryl Castle, for all her
support and encouragement during the planning and writing of this
book, and for the many hours she has spent acting as a chauffeur
whilst I walked the numerous long distance paths in the South-East.

First published 1990 by
A & C Black (Publishers) Ltd
35 Bedford Row, London WC1R 4JH

© 1990 Alan Castle

ISBN 0 7136 3261 5

A CIP catalogue record for this book is available
from the British Library.

Printed and bound in Great Britain by
BPCC Wheatons Ltd, Exeter.

CONTENTS

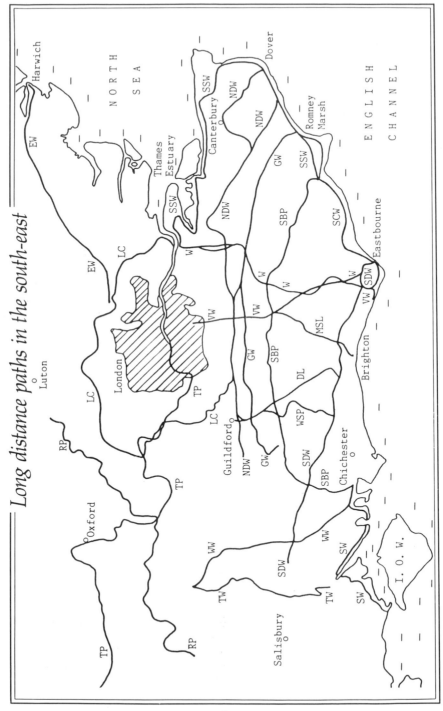

Long distance paths in the south-east

INTRODUCTION

They only know a country who are acquainted with its footpaths. By the roads, indeed, the outside may be seen; but the footpaths go through the heart of the land.
Richard Jefferies
1848–87

The rights of way network: a national asset to be enjoyed

Many walkers living in the South-East regularly travel hundreds of miles to the National Parks and other upland areas of Britain, without realising that the region in which they live also possesses fine walking country. In lowland Britain there is an interlacing network of long distance paths (LDPs) threading through a variety of landscapes; chalk downland and greensand hills, meadow and orchard, ancient forest and deciduous woodland, heritage coast, sandy heath and landscaped parkland. Walkers living in the north and west of the country may perhaps not consider the South-East a suitable area for a walking holiday, thinking of it merely as a large urban sprawl. They would be wrong; there is more to Britain than mountains and moors, the gentle hills and wooded vales of the South-East presenting some of the most captivating and tranquil scenery in all Britain. True, there are no rocky mountain tops or high, desolate moors; the charm of this land is perhaps more subtle, in its own way just as enticing as the hills of upland Britain. This is why such a large percentage of this corner of England has been designated as Areas of Outstanding Natural Beauty (q.v.) representing some of the finest scenery in lowland Britain, rich in bird and plant life as well as being home for badger, deer and other mammals.

The many hundreds of miles of LDPs in the South-East are virtually on the doorstep of the large number of people living within a 70-mile radius of the capital. These rights of way are part of our great national heritage, there to be used by everyone, not just the dedicated long distance walker, but also the day rambler, jogger, birdwatcher and botanist; even for walking the dog. In years gone by they served a very practical function, providing the means of reaching church, school, farm

Key to map opposite

DL	*Downs Link*	RP	*Ridgeway Path*	TP	*Thames Path*
EW	*Essex Way*	SBP	*Sussex Border Path*	TW	*Test Way*
GW	*Greensand Way*	SCW	*South Coast Way*	VW	*Vanguard Way*
LC	*London Countryway*	SDW	*South Downs Way*	W	*Wealdway*
MSL	*Mid-Sussex Link*	SSW	*Saxon Shore Way*	WSP	*Wey-South Path*
NDW	*North Downs Way*	SW	*Solent Way*	WW	*Wayfarer's Walk*

and field, and allowing pilgrims and others passage through a land fraught with dangers from man and beast. Today they have been super-seded by our modern road system, but remain, at the very least, as a treasured leisure facility. But they are far more than this; they are the means of penetrating to the heart of the land, to absorb the countryside and so enrich one's life. The cost and effort of maintaining this network of paths is considerable, but the enormous benefits of health and well-being that the system can bring to everyone have prompted the Countryside Commission to declare the intention of opening up all 140 000 miles of rights of way in England and Wales by the end of the century.

Research by the Countryside Commission has indicated that many people are unsure of their rights in the countryside and timid in their approach to public footpaths. There is therefore a need for clearer signposting of public rights of way in the countryside. The development of a network of LDPs is helping in this respect. The indication on the ground of a clearly waymarked route bearing a distinctive symbol helps to entice people to explore the countryside on foot. The arguments against waymarking rarely apply in lowland Britain where the novice walker is unlikely to be led into dangerous terrain. Clear but unobtrusive waymarking will help to direct people along rights of way, so ensuring that they are walked more frequently. If our paths are not used they will at best become overgrown and obstructed; at worst they will be lost for ever.

It is ironic that many paths in the National Parks, which are located in low-populated regions of England and Wales, are suffering from problems of erosion, whereas other rights of way close to large centres of population are invisible on the ground, obstructed and difficult to follow. Again, research by the Countryside Commission has indicated that lack of information is a major reason why people do not venture into unfamiliar countryside. However, there is plenty of information available on the many LDPs in the South-East, as this book demon-strates, and by using these routes the walker will not only discover new, richly rewarding areas but will also help in 'spreading the load', alleviating the problems of erosion in the more popular areas. Even the South-East has its erosion problems in such places as Box Hill and in the Seven Sisters Country Park. Why go to these places time and again, pleasant as they are, when there is so much more to discover along the many other paths in the area? In so doing one is helping to keep the network open. The author walked the entire length of the Sussex Border Path in a series of day walks over a period of 18 months. Although he always walked at weekends, he met no other walkers on the route. This can be compared with many parts of the South Downs where hundreds flock every day of the year. The South-East has much more to offer than the South Downs. This book is an invitation to explore further. There is enough walking described here to keep even the most enthusiastic of walkers content for a very long time.

Classification of long distance paths

A misconception often held, even by seasoned walkers, is that the only LDPs in Britain are the Official ones, now called National Trails, such as the Pennine Way and Offa's Dyke Path, developed, funded and maintained by the Countryside Commission. There are 14 of these in the country, although more are planned, whereas there are several hundred other recognised long distance routes throughout the land, ranging from ten to several hundred miles in length. These can be crudely classified as follows (the 17 LDPs, total mileage 1708 miles, featured in this book have been included as examples).

1 National Trails. The new term for Official Long Distance Paths. They are the responsibility of the Countryside Commission. New rights of way often have to be designated for these paths to be established. They are all waymarked with distinctive acorn symbols. Examples: North Downs Way, Ridgeway Path, South Downs Way, Thames Path; 4 routes, total mileage 521 miles.

2 County Council LDPs. Developed, waymarked and usually maintained by the various county councils or local authorities. Occasionally, very short sections of new rights of way have to be designated to complete these paths. They are all waymarked with a specific and distinctive symbol. Examples: Downs Link, Saxon Shore Way, Solent Way, Wayfarer's Walk, Test Way; 5 routes, total mileage 348 miles.

3 Routes planned and developed by various walking or environmental organisations. Rarely are new rights of way necessary to establish these paths. Many, but not all, have a distinctive waymark symbol. In time some of these LDPs become adopted by the relevant county councils, e.g. Essex Way and Greensand Way (Surrey). Examples: Greensand Way and Wealdway (Ramblers' Association), London Countryway (Long Distance Walkers Association), Vanguard Way (Vanguards Rambling Club), Essex Way (Council for the Protection of Rural England); 5 routes, total mileage 535 miles.

4 Routes devised and published by individuals or small groups of people. These paths always link existing rights of way. They usually bear no distinctive waymark symbol. Examples: South Coast Way, Sussex Border Path, Wey-South Path; 3 routes, total mileage 304 miles.

The LDPs under categories 2, 3 and 4 (sometimes referred to

erroneously as Unofficial) were for a long time placed under the some-what vague generic title of Recreational Path. The Countryside Commission has suggested the term Regional Route for those paths under categories 2 and 3.

The LDPs featured in this book sample all the varied terrain and landscape found in lowland Britain. They include downland escarpments, heath, wood and headland, coastal path and parkland, disused railway track, canal, reservoir and river bank. Most of the County Tops in the South-East are visited, including the highest point in the region on top of Leith Hill Tower in Surrey, at 1000 ft (305 m) above sea level. Of the 17 LDPs described in this book, 3 are primarily downland walks, 1 follows a greensand ridge, 1 is a walk along a disused railway track, 1 takes the course of an old canal, 2 follow major rivers, 3 are coastal walks, 1 traces a county boundary, 2 cross the Kent/Sussex Weald, 1 circumnavigates the capital and the remaining 2 cross entire counties. A tremendous variety of landscapes and themes. Something for everyone.

The cost of developing the various categories of LDP varies enormously, from many hundreds of thousands of pounds for building bridges and stiles and negotiating new rights of way (e.g. the Thames Path) to the cost of producing a small booklet, as in the case of many of the routes devised by individuals, linking existing rights of way. It is hoped that readers will gain an apprenticeship on some of the LDPs described in this book and use their acquired knowledge and experience to devise their own long distance cross-country routes. The basic material, i.e. the 140 000 miles of rights of way in this country, is at everyone's disposal; walking them and publishing your efforts, in whatever form, will help to keep this network used and open. Readers contemplating this should first contact the LDPAS (see Useful Addresses) for advice on avoiding over-used areas and where the proposed route may duplicate any others. The best long distance routes satisfy two criteria: they traverse attractive and varied terrain and are scenically of a high quality; and they have a theme, such as following an ancient trade route, walking an abandoned railway, or linking two historic towns.

Day walks or multi-day holidays

There are 3 principal ways in which the LDPs featured in this book can be accomplished.

1   As *continuous holidays* walking the whole or part of a path. This is the conventional method of walking such a trail and there is no doubt that this option affords the greatest sense of achievement. In unprepared walkers or those who plan to accomplish too great a distance each day, it can also bring the most hardship and suffering. If a blister or sprain

occurs on such a walk it can sometimes ruin the holiday. All of the LDPs in this book can be walked in this way. Several of them make fine 1 or 2 week holidays. It is the best method to use on those paths which present transport problems along the way. The South Downs Way, North Downs Way, Ridgeway Path and Wealdway are particularly suited to this type of walking holiday.

It is of course not necessary to walk the entire length of one LDP during a walking holiday. An interesting way of using the network is to link two or more LDPs together to form one's own itinerary. Inspection of the map on page 4 will reveal numerous possibilities of varying length. For example, a large circuit can be made from Eastbourne using the South Downs Way, Downs Link, North Downs Way or Greensand Way, and Vanguard Way or Wealdway. In Hampshire a thorough exploration of the county can be made by linking together the Wayfarer's Walk, Test Way and Solent Way. All the information necessary to plan such trips will be found in this book under the Information sections of each LDP.

2   In *day stages* over a period of time. With this method there are no problems of finding accommodation at the end of each day's walk. However, it can sometimes be difficult to return home or to the car after the section has been walked. These problems can be overcome by a variety of techniques: i) Arrange to be taken by car to the start of each section and collected at the finish point at the end of the day. ii) Use two cars. Drive both to the finish of the stage and leave car number 1 there. In car number 2 drive to the start. Walk the route and drive back in car 1 to pick up car 2. Obviously at least two drivers are required for this system. iii) Liaise with friends. Party number 1 goes by car to point A on the LDP and walks from A to B. Party number 2 goes by car to point B and walks B to A. Car keys are exchanged on meeting. iv) Devise a circular route walking a section of the LDP, returning to the car or railway station by alternative rights of way. v) Walk each stage 'there and back'. The views can look quite different when walking in the opposite direction and things missed on the outward journey may be seen on the return.

The day walks method is best reserved for those paths which have day stages between railway stations or are in areas having good public transport. Those paths particularly suited to this method are the London Countryway, Saxon Shore Way, Solent Way, South Coast Way and the Thames Path.

3   Over a *weekend* or *long weekend*. Some of the shorter routes can be walked over a weekend or bank holiday weekend. Those most suited to this approach are the Downs Link, Wey-South Path, Vanguard Way and Test Way.

4   From a *base*, e.g. a holiday cottage, returning each night. The problems here are similar to those listed under point 2 above.

Help for novice walkers

No previous experience of rambling is necessary to walk the LDPs in the South-East. However, those who are unfamiliar with walking in the countryside would do well to start slowly with day walks until fitness, confidence and the ability to use map, compass and guidebook have been acquired. It is important not to overestimate one's ability and to misjudge how far one may comfortably walk in a day. This is particularly important when accommodation has been booked for a number of consecutive nights. Remember that time will be taken up visiting places of interest, having lunch, etc. Do not make the mistake of considering these walks as feats of endurance. They are there to be savoured and enjoyed.

For those who may feel daunted at starting out on their own, there are many walking clubs and organisations who regularly hike these paths, either as day walks or as walking holidays. Both the Ramblers' Association and the Long Distance Walkers Association (see Useful Addresses) have local groups in all regions of the South-East. By joining one of these groups or any of the other walking clubs (details from public libraries), the novice will be able to learn the rudiments of map reading and gain confidence in following a route in the countryside. These clubs consist of like-minded people; friendships will flourish and companions will be found for walking the LDPs. Another option is to gain experience on some of the many guided walks organised by the various county councils. Several of the county councils in the South-East have guided walks programmes. Current details can be obtained from the relevant county council offices (see Useful Addresses). Finally, certain commercial concerns offer walking holidays along some of the LDPs, where transport and accommodation are provided. Their advertisements frequently appear in the walking press, in magazines such as *The Great Outdoors*.

Areas of Outstanding Natural Beauty and Heritage Coasts

Most members of the public are aware of the National Parks of Britain, protected areas of mountain, moorland and rocky coast, all of which (with the exception of the relatively new Broads Authority) lie to the north or west of England and Wales. However, far fewer people are cognisant of the many designated Areas of Outstanding Natural Beauty (AONBs) throughout England and Wales. AONBs generally lack extensive areas of open country as in the National Parks, but nevertheless, as their rather clumsy title suggests, they contain such fine areas of natural beauty that it is deemed in the national interest to protect them from unsuitable future developments and allocate funds and resources to conserve their character. It is the responsibility of the Countryside Commission to identify and designate such areas and define their boundaries. Since 1956 the Countryside Commission has confirmed 38 AONBs, amounting to nearly 13 per cent of the total area of England and Wales, spread throughout many regions of both upland and lowland Britain.

The South-East is fortunate in possessing several AONBs, an indication of the outstanding landscape in the region. There are 11 AONBs in the area covered by this book. These are in the Kent Downs, High Weald, Sussex Downs, Surrey Hills, East Hampshire, Chichester Harbour, South Hampshire Coast, North Wessex Downs, Cotswolds, Chilterns and Dedham Vale. There is an enormous variety of landscape within the boundaries of these areas, from chalk downland to mature deciduous woodland, from coastal mudflats and marshland to sandy heaths; they represent some of the finest areas of lowland Britain. Discussion in the late 1980s focused on the suggestion that two of these, the South Downs and the Chilterns, should be elevated to the status of National Parks. Indeed the South Downs was on the original list drawn up by the old National Parks Commission back in the early 1950s. More information can be found in the AONB Directory obtainable from Countryside Commission Publications (see Useful Addresses).

Heritage Coasts are afforded protection similar to that provided for AONBs. They represent the most scenically outstanding stretches of undeveloped coast and like AONBs are defined and designated by the Countryside Commission. There are some 44 Heritage Coasts in England and Wales, but unfortunately the South-East only boasts three: South-Foreland, Dover–Folkestone and the Sussex Heritage Coast. The first two include the famous White Cliffs of Dover and the Sussex Heritage Coast embraces Beachy Head and the cliffs of the Seven Sisters. These magnificent coasts are of vital importance as some of the last undeveloped coastline in the South-East.

All of the AONBs and Heritage Coasts in the South-East are covered by the 17 LDPs featured in this book. Several of the routes run entirely within AONBs. All of the LDPs described in this book pass through at least one AONB and several include sections of Heritage Coast.

Equipment

No specialist equipment is required to walk these paths. They can be walked in all seasons and in all weathers (within reason). Some form of waterproof should always be carried, although an expensive garment designed primarily for hill country is not necessary. The humble umbrella is much undervalued as an item of equipment for the walker. Many of the paths on these routes are muddy, especially between October and April away from the downland areas, and a pair of light-weight walking boots is therefore the recommended form of footwear. During high summer some paths become dry and hard underfoot and in these conditions a pair of good-quality trainers may be preferable to boots. A rucksack will be required, the size of which will depend on whether the outing is a day walk or part of a walking holiday. A small first-aid kit to treat any cuts and scratches is also advisable. The rest is mainly a matter of common sense and trial and error. The most important point of all is to keep the pack as light as possible. The walk is to be enjoyed, not endured.

Maps and navigation

Oddly, as many experienced walkers know, route finding in lowland areas, with fences, hedgerows and confined footpaths to contend with, can be even more difficult than in upland regions. Hence large-scale maps (such as the O.S. 1:25 000 Pathfinder or Outdoor Leisure Maps) are often more useful than those in the 1:50 000 Landranger series. However, it is worth considering the following points.

1   Many Pathfinder sheets are required to walk one LDP. This is therefore an expensive solution.

2   The exact routes of LDPs are not marked on either Landranger or Pathfinder maps. National Trails are overlaid on Outdoor Leisure Maps, although the only one of interest in the South-East is the Brighton and Sussex Vale Outdoor Leisure Map showing part of the South Downs Way.

3   Both Landranger and Second Series Pathfinder Maps show rights of way but note that the old First Series Pathfinder Maps lack this informa-

tion. Most of the Second Series Pathfinders are double sheets showing twice the area of the First Series.

The best solution for walking these LDPs is to purchase one of the recommended guidebooks which usually have detailed sketch maps of the route together with a route description. Transfer the route, if you wish, on to the relevant O.S. Landranger sheets. It is important to carry a map as well as a guidebook for two reasons: i) it enables the route to be rejoined if a mistake is made and the LDP temporarily lost; ii) it allows an appreciation of the surrounding area and helps in identifying landmarks. A guidebook is useful not only for following the route, but for providing information on places of interest on and off route, transport and accommodation, etc.

In order to provide some idea of the navigational difficulties of each route, a simple grading system has been used in this book. None of the LDPs described can be considered hazardous or difficult, but some are easier to follow than others.

Grade A   Well waymarked and usually quite straightforward to follow. Ideal for first-timers.

Grade B   Can be difficult to follow in some areas, but few major problems.

Grade C   Navigation can be tedious in places. Waymarking is sometimes poor or absent.

The book contains 5 LDPs at Grade A, 8 at Grade B, 3 at Grade C and 1 graded B/C. These grades are in no way official, but are merely an indication of the difficulties, if any, that are likely to be encountered. The novice walker is advised to start with an A-grade walk, or at most a B-grade path. After gaining confidence the C-grade LDPs should present no serious problems.

Most of the LDPs featured in this book have distinctive waymarks, but a few are not signposted as such, although the footpaths and bridleways used are usually marked with yellow and blue conventional arrows. It is a fact of walking life that waymarks often appear where they are not needed, e.g. in the centre of villages, and yet are often absent where most required, e.g. in the middle of a wood or complex field system. The law only requires the local authority to signpost public rights of way where they leave a public road and this is often the reason for this frustating situation.

Distances and altitudes are given in miles and feet respectively, because most people are familiar with this system, but also in kilometres and metres because this is how they appear on modern O.S. maps.

Transport and accommodation

It will probably be necessary to make use of public transport at some stage, whether returning to the car left at the day's starting point if walking the path in separate stages, or to get to and from the start/finish of a walking holiday. The South-East is fortunate in having what is probably the most extensive public transport network in the whole of the country. Despite the Beeching cuts of the mid-1960s, Network South-East of British Rail still has a fairly extensive branch line network. Certain services are likely to be improved when the Channel Tunnel has been completed. Although bus services to rural areas have steadily declined during the last two decades, the deregulation of the late 1980s may lead to a slightly improved situation. A few bus companies and local authorities operate a 'rambler bus' during the most popular summer weekends. Since walking is becoming a more popular pursuit, more of these services may be seen in the future. It is advisable to check bus and train timetables and itineraries before setting out on a walking trip. Remember that services are often inferior on Sundays. British Rail enquiries and the telephone numbers of the major bus companies operating in the area are listed under Useful Addresses at the end of the book. An invaluable booklet is 'Scenic England and Wales by Bus', which gives details, on a county-by-county basis, of the rural bus companies and the areas they serve. The publication, supported by the Countryside Commission, is available free from Transport Marketing Ltd, 4 Station Road, Knowle, Solihull, West Midlands B93 OHT.

Unless the LDPs are walked strictly as a series of day walks, then some form of accommodation will be required at the end of each day. Most people will probably seek bed and breakfast, but use can also be made of youth hostels where other walkers and outdoor types will be encountered. There are many camp sites in the region, although rarely on the route at the required intervals. It is not easy to camp wild in the South-East; permission should always be sought from the landowner.

A useful publication is the *Rambler's Yearbook and Accommodation Guide* published by the Ramblers' Association. It is updated annually and is free to members, but can also be purchased by non-members. It contains details, addresses and telephone numbers of bed and breakfast establishments and hotels which welcome walkers, and indicates those which are on or near to a recognised LDP. The YHA's *Accommodation Guide* provides details of youth hostels in the area. The South-East England Tourist Board offers two useful Where to Stay publications entitled *Hotels, Motels and Guest Houses* and *Farmhouses, Bed and Breakfast, Inns and Hostels*. Finally, local Tourist Information Centres will provide details of accommodation available in their areas. The addresses and telephone numbers of all the many centres throughout the South-East are listed in the brochure 'Tourist Information Centres in Britain' available free of charge from the English Tourist Board. All of the organisations mentioned above are listed under Useful Addresses.

Specific details of both transport and accommodation change rapidly and so it is essential to check and make arrangements prior to walking an LDP. The preliminary planning of a walking trip should not be considered a chore. It is all part and parcel of walking a long distance route and a certain sense of achievement is gained from working out the logistics of a walk and successfully executing the plan.

Other facilities such as shops, pubs and cafés will also be sought by wayfarers. Unlike many of the well-known LDPs in remote areas (such as the Pennine Way) most of the paths covered in this book frequently encounter villages and towns where these facilities may be found. A good pub lunch is part of the enjoyment of this type of walking. Take care to remove muddy boots before entering such establishments.

Achievement badges

Cloth badges are available for the various long distance paths in the South-East and these can be purchased when the walk has been completed. Collecting these provides added interest to long distance walking. They may be sewn onto rucksacks or tracksuits, or collected in an album. Some walkers have devised novel ways of collecting and presenting them. For instance, one walker has sewn them on to a rug which will eventually become a family heirloom. There are badges available for all of the LDPs featured in this book. One of the main suppliers is P & R Publicity (see Useful Addresses).

The South Downs Way

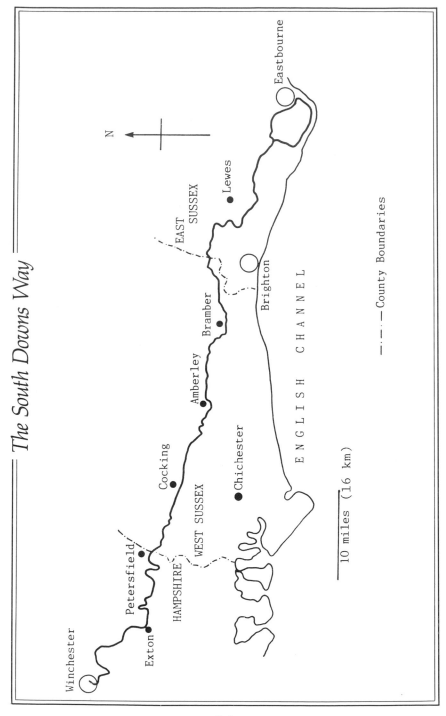

Winchester
Exton
Petersfield
HAMPSHIRE
WEST SUSSEX
Cocking
Chichester
Amberley
Bramber
EAST SUSSEX
Lewes
Brighton
Eastbourne
N
ENGLISH CHANNEL
10 miles (16 km)
— · — County Boundaries

LONG DISTANCE PATHS

The South Downs Way

Information

Length	102 miles (164 km)
Start & finish	Eastbourne (Grid ref. TV 600972 or TV 598983)
	Winchester (Grid ref. SU 483293)
Details of route	Eastbourne – Alfriston – Rodmell – Falmer –
	Pyecombe – Upper Beeding – Washington –
	Houghton – Cocking – Buriton – Exton –
	Winchester
Counties traversed	East Sussex, West Sussex and Hampshire
Nature of route	National Trail. Managed and funded by the
	Countryside Commission. The first (and by 1990
	still the only) 'official' long distance bridleway.
	Therefore it can be followed on horseback or by
	bicycle as well as on foot. The whole length of the
	Hampshire Extension will also be a bridleway once
	the route has been officially opened
Accepted abbreviation	SDW
Average duration	One week
Landscape	Chalk downland
AONBs & Heritage Coast	The SDW runs for its entire length through Areas of
	Outstanding Natural Beauty, viz. the Sussex Downs
	AONB and the East Hampshire AONB. The
	footpath alternative is along the Sussex Heritage
	Coast and passes through the Seven Sisters Country
	Park
Date of opening	15 July 1972 (Eastbourne to Buriton, 80 miles;
	129 km). The Hampshire Extension from Buriton to
	Winchester is due for completion some time in the
	early 1990s
Waymarking	The Countryside Commission acorn symbol. The
	waymarking in East Sussex is mainly by low-level
	concrete plinths, whilst that in West Sussex consists
	predominantly of wooden fingerposts. New
	waymarks are to be erected along the Hampshire
	Extension
Navigation	Grade A
Maps	O.S. Landranger 1:50 000, Nos 185, 197, 198, 199
	O.S. Pathfinder 1:25 000, Nos SU: 61/71, 81/91;
	TQ: 01/11, 21/31, 00/10, 20/30, 40/50; TV:
	49/59/69 (these cover the route from Buriton to
	Eastbourne)
	OS Outdoor Leisure Map 1:25 000: Brighton & the

Sussex Vale. This useful map covers the section from Kingston near Lewes (after Rodmell) to Upper Beeding

Alternative routes

There is an alternative route (footpath only) from Eastbourne to Alfriston via Beachy Head and the Seven Sisters Country Park at the eastern end of the Trail. This is highly recommended. It is 2 miles (3.2 km) longer than the bridleway via Jevington

Shared LDPs

The Wealdway shares the bridleway route of the SDW for about a mile in the vicinity of Willingdon Hill, near Eastbourne

Other LDPs

The Downs Link starts/finishes on the SDW just north of St Botolph's Church near Upper Beeding. The Wey-South Path meets the SDW to the south of the village of Amberley. The South Coast Way links with the SDW at Eastbourne. The Sussex Border Path intersects the SDW near South Harting, a few miles from Petersfield. Finally, the Vanguard Way crosses the SDW at Alfriston

Transport

Consult the South Downs Way Public Transport Guide obtainable from West Sussex County Council (see Useful Addresses). There is a British Rail main line station at Eastbourne as well as buses and car parks. Buriton has a frequent bus service and a car park. The nearest British Rail station to Buriton is at Petersfield, about 3 miles (5 km) from Buriton. Winchester has buses, car parks and a main line British Rail station

Accommodation

There are youth hostels at Beachy Head, Alfriston, Telscombe (2 miles (3 km) off route), Truleigh Hill, Arundel (4 miles (6 km) off route) and Winchester. Many villages on or near the route offer B & B accommodation

Guidebooks

1   *Along the South Downs Way and on to Winchester* by the Eastbourne Rambling Club. 64 pages. Still the best and cheapest practical guide to the SDW. Detailed route descriptions (both ways) of the official route from Eastbourne to Buriton and of a provisional route from Buriton to Winchester. The booklet includes the historical background to the Trail and also a guide to accommodation (B & B addresses). The guide, which is regularly updated, is illustrated with a small number of black and white photographs and with sketch maps of each section of the walk. It can be obtained locally, from the Ramblers' Association or direct from the Eastbourne Rambling Club (see Useful Addresses). The proceeds of the sale of the book go to the South Downs

Preservation Society. Recommended.
2   *A Guide to the South Downs Way* by Miles Jebb
(1984), Constable. 332 pages. Hardback. The route is
described in both directions in 15 stages between
Eastbourne and Winchester. Extensions and
excursions are also described viz. the Lewes Loop,
Arundel Loop, Petworth Spur, Lavant Loop and
Stansted Spur. A series of appendices outlines the
geology and prehistory of the Downs, downland
farming and principal downland wildflowers. There
is a large number of black and white photographs.
3   *The South Downs Way* by Sean Jennett (1978,
revised 1984). HMSO. 112 pages. The 'official'
guidebook covering the original route from
Eastbourne to Buriton. It includes O.S. 1:25 000
maps with the route of the SDW clearly marked.
Note added when going to press. The new National
Trail Guide to the SDW by Paul Millmore, a South
Downs Conservation Officer, has now been
published. It follows the same format as the other
National Trail Guides in the series.
4   *Walking on the North and South Downs* by Mark
Chapman (1985), Robert Hale. 190 pages. The book
contains sketch maps and a route description of
almost the entire SDW (from west to east). It also
includes several circular walks based on the SDW.
Illustrated with a small collection of black and white
photographs.
5   *The South Downs Way and the Downs Link* by Kev
Reynolds (1989), Cicerone Press. 136 pages. The
SDW is described in 12 daily stages from
Eastbourne to Buriton and 2 stages for the SDW
Extension (Buriton to Exton and Exton to
Winchester). The route is also described in the
reverse direction (Winchester to Eastbourne) and the
two alternative routes between Eastbourne and
Alfriston are included. The book contains
photographs and sketch maps as well as the author's
personal reflections.
6   *The South Downs Way*. South East England
Tourist Board Guide. The route is divided into
convenient sections and there are details of
accommodation. Not a full guide. Available from the
South East Tourist Board.

*Shorter walks based
on the SDW*

There are several publications describing circular day
walks using sections of the SDW. The following is a
selection.
1   *On Foot in East Sussex*. An Eastbourne Rambling

Club publication. Contains about 27 circular walks (from 4.5 to 14 miles; 7.2 to 22.5 km). Regularly updated.
2   *South Downs Walks for Motorists* by Ben Perkins. F. Warne. 99 pages. 30 circular walks from 3.5 to 9 miles (5.6 to 14.5 km).
3   *The Ordnance Survey Leisure Guide, South Downs* (1989). Walks and drives and general tourist information.

Guided walks

Every year it is usual for various guided walks along the SDW to be organised by walking clubs and other organisations. Coach transport is often provided to convey walkers back to the start of a section of the Way. Often the whole length of the SDW can be walked in this way. Details of these ventures are often given in the national walking press

Description

The SDW is probably the most well known of all the LDPs in the South-East. It is one of the six LDPs that were originally recommended in the report *Footpaths and Access to the Countryside* produced by the Hobhouse Committee back in 1947. Ironically, although the Hobhouse Committee recommended the establishment of a route from Beachy Head along the South Downs to Winchester, the original path opened in 1972 (the fifth Official LDP to be opened in England and Wales) ran only as far as Buriton, just over the Hampshire border. It has taken numerous organisations nearly twenty years to persuade the Countryside Commission to extend the path to its logical termination at Winchester, the county town of Hampshire and 'capital' of Wessex.

The SDW, now a National Trail, is one of three LDPs in the South-East that follow ranges of chalk downland, the others being the North Downs and the Ridgeway (q.v.). Of the three escarpments the South Downs is the most continuous, running almost unbroken from the sea cliffs at Beachy Head for almost 100 miles (161 km) throughout the length of Sussex and well into Hampshire, finally petering out before Winchester. The SDW is a true hilltop path, keeping to the heights as much as possible, descending only to cross one of the four river valleys (Cuckmere, Ouse, Adur and Arun) or one of the four dry valleys which breach the escarpment connecting the Weald with the coastal plain. The South Downs are the highlands of the South-East, although nowhere do they exceed 900 ft (275 m). Butser Hill (889 ft; 271 m) in Hampshire on the SDW Extension is the highest point on the South Downs. Ditchling

The lighthouse beneath the chalk cliffs of Beachy Head. Built in 1902, it stands 142 feet (12.8 m) high and its light is visible for up to 16 miles (25.7 km)

Beacon at 813 ft (248 m) is the 'county top' of East Sussex. The highest point on the South Downs in West Sussex is Teglease (836 ft; 255 m) near Cocking. Despite their relatively low height these hills provide excellent viewpoints over the Weald and out over the coastal plain to the English Channel. The northern escarpment is often steep, as for example above Fulking, whereas to the south the hills descend more gently towards the coast.

The 'blunt, bowheaded, whalebacked Downs' as Kipling called them, fringe the sea in the east, but in the west are separated by a flat coastal strip which widens as it proceeds westwards. The east and west Downs are quite different in character and this is evident when walking the SDW as a continuous walk. In the east the Downs are bare, smooth rolling hills, whereas the western Downs are often heavily wooded. Beech is the predominant tree and beech hangers are common, reaching down the hillsides to the valleys.

Man has had a tremendous effect on the topography of these hills. In prehistoric times he cleared woodland and built hill forts and burial chambers. Later he learnt that grass will grow easily in the poor, thin soil overlaying the chalk and so he used the Downs for large-scale sheep rearing from the fourteenth century onwards for the medieval wool industry. In the heyday of the eighteenth and nineteenth centuries there were up to 250 000 sheep on the Downs between the Ouse and Beachy Head. The area was famous for the Southdown breed of sheep and the tinkle of sheep bells would have accompanied any walker on the Downs in those days. Sheep remained on the Downs until World War II when

Belle Tout Lighthouse on the cliffs above Birling Gap on the South Downs Way. Built inside an Iron Age enclosure in 1831, today it is a private residence

The cliffs near Beachy Head. The footpath alternative of the South Downs Way treads the short downland turf along this Heritage Coast

radar masts and searchlights were erected on the summits as the Battle of Britain was fought in the skies. Extensive cultivation followed the war and the less economic sheep were removed. However, the springy turf characteristic of downland is still very common on these hills and makes for splendid walking.

Even the most unaware of walkers will soon notice that the Downs are chalk hills. The chalk is very close to the surface and many of the routes across the Downs are ancient, white, eroded tracks. The walker will also soon realise that there is no water on these hills. Chalk is porous and rapidly absorbs rainwater, which comes to the surface as springs where the chalk meets clay or sandstone. A good example of this is the gushing spring in Fulking below the SDW north of Shoreham. It is for this reason that villages are often found along the foot of the northern escarpment, wherever there is a spring. The alkaline chalk favours calcium-loving flowers and before the widespread use of pesticides, a number of flowers were very common on the Downs. Cowslips were very abundant in the spring and wild thyme gave a pleasant aroma to the air during the summer months. Sheep grazing and cultivation have prevented the natural flora of the Downs from developing, but today there are several small nature reserves, many of which are passed on the SDW, where the land is being allowed to revert to its natural state. Birdlife is represented by lapwings, seagulls and kestrels, but the most well remembered will be the lark, often seen and heard above the escarpment.

Where there is chalk there is also flint, and indeed Sussex is richer in this material than any other part of Britain. For centuries flint was the most common form of building material in an area where stone and brick were scarce. Witness to this is seen in the many fine downland churches observed from the SDW as well as in numerous farm buildings and cottages.

The SDW can, like all the other routes in this book, be walked in either direction, but perhaps the majority start in Eastbourne. From here the footpath over the Seven Sisters is recommended in preference to the bridleway via Jevington. For day walkers the circular route formed by the footpath and bridleway from Eastbourne to Alfriston is one of the classic walks in the South-East, although it is a very long day (about 20 miles; 32 km). The footpath begins at the edge of the Downs at Eastbourne, climbs to Beachy Head (from the French Beau Chef – beautiful head) and then follows springy downland turf over the chalk cliffs of the Seven Sisters. The scenery is magnificent hereabouts and includes a view of the oxbow curves at Cuckmere Haven. The route continues through the picturesque village of West Dean and on through Friston Forest to reach Litlington by the River Cuckmere. The inland bridleway route via Willingdon Hill, Jevington and Windover Hill is

The Seven Sisters Country Park was purchased by East Sussex Council in 1971

The Tiger Inn at East Dean. Dating from the 13th century, it stands on the picturesque village green

Friston Church. This downland church is situated near an attractive pond on a hill to the west of the village of East Dean

met at Plonk Barn and the SDW then goes over the footbridge into Alfriston.

Alfriston is a justly famous village, having some fine timbered inns and the enormous church known as the Cathedral of the South Downs. Next to the church is a fine old Clergy House, which is distinguished as being the first building acquired by the National Trust — in 1896 for £10. From Alfriston the Way climbs gradually to Firle Beacon (713 ft; 218 m) and then across the Downs to descend to the second river valley, that of the Ouse. After the pretty village of Southease and its Norman church, the SDW climbs over Iford Hill and descends to Newmarket Inn on the A27, a few miles to the west of Lewes, the county town of East Sussex. A detour to the ancient town of Lewes, with its Norman castle and house in which Anne of Cleves lived, is strongly recommended.

`The SDW meanwhile crosses Plumpton Plain and continues over the fine viewpoint of Ditchling Beacon to approach Jack and Jill windmills, famous landmarks hereabouts. After Pyecombe and Saddlescombe the Way climbs up to Devil's Dyke, a famous tourist spot which once boasted a small railway. The Dyke is said to be the result of the work of the devil. Legend has it that he was disturbed whilst digging a trench in the Downs in order to flood the Weald and its churches. The next major landmark is Chanctonbury Ring, beloved of the composer John Ireland who lived nearby. Alas, several of the trees on the Ring were badly damaged in the hurricane of October 1987. The route continues over Chantry Hill to descend to Amberley railway station in the Arun valley. Here is the Chalk Pits Museum which is well worth a visit. A detour to Arundel with castle, cathedral and Wildfowl Trust is recommended here.

The Way climbs from Houghton, where Charles II is reputed to have stayed at the George and Dragon when fleeing to France, to pass to the south of the Roman villa at Bignor (open to the public) and cross the old Roman road of Stane Street. After Grafton Down the route descends to the A286 north of Singleton, the home of the splendid Weald and Downland Open Air Museum. Here many fine, traditional buildings have been saved, re-erected and restored. The countryside becomes increasingly wooded as the SDW traverses Linch and Harting Downs to cross the West Sussex/Hampshire border near Buriton. From here the new 20 mile (32.2 km) extension of the SDW continues to Winchester.

From the Queen Elizabeth Country Park the path climbs to Butser Hill, an iron age hill fort, and on to the village of Exton. The final section of downland is traversed over Beacon Hill, another hill fort, and on to Cheesefoot Head. After Telegraph Hill the SDW skirts a rifle range and descends to cross the River Itchen into Winchester. This city with its fine cathedral and many historical associations is a fitting end to a classic walk.

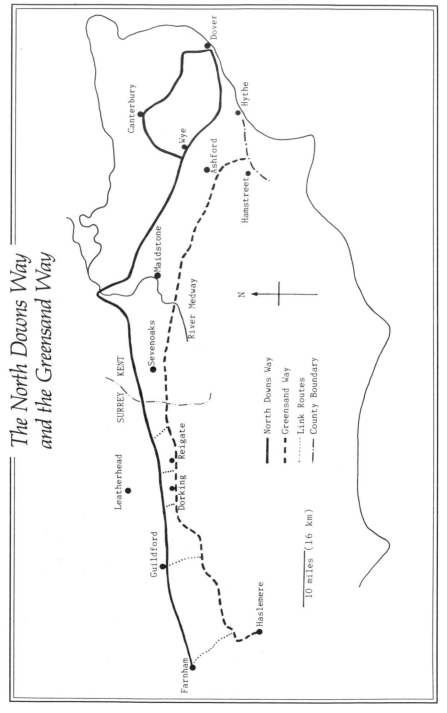

The North Downs Way and the Greensand Way

Dover
Canterbury
Hythe
Wye
Ashford
Hamstreet
Maidstone
River Medway
SURREY KENT
Sevenoaks
Leatherhead
Reigate
Dorking
Guildford
Haslemere
Farnham

N

North Downs Way
Greensand Way
Link Routes
County Boundary

10 miles (16 km)

The North Downs Way

Information

Length	Total: 153.5 miles (247.1 km)
	Farnham to Boughton Lees: 97.5 miles (157 km)
	Boughton Lees to Dover via Folkestone: 24 miles (38.6 km)
	Boughton Lees to Dover via Canterbury: 32 miles (51.5 km)
	Hence, Farnham to Dover via Folkestone: 121.5 miles (195.6 km) and, Farnham to Dover via Canterbury: 129.5 miles (208.5 km)
Start & finish	Farnham (Grid ref. SU 844468)
	Dover (Grid ref. TR 319417)
Details of route	Farnham – Guildford – Dorking – Merstham – Otford – Wrotham – River Medway – Charing – Boughton Lees – (Wye) – (Canterbury) – Dover
Counties traversed	Surrey and Kent
Nature of route	National Trail. Managed and funded by the Countryside Commission
Accepted abbreviation	NDW
Average duration	10–12 days
Landscape	Chalk downland. Woods, sandy tracks, orchards, farmland, towns and coast
AONBs & Heritage Coast	Almost the entire route of the NDW passes through Areas of Outstanding Natural Beauty, viz. the Surrey Hills AONB and the Kent Downs AONB. The Dover–Folkstone Heritage Coast is met at the eastern end of the trail
Date of opening	30 September 1978 by Dr Donald Coggan, Archbishop of Canterbury, at a ceremony on Broad Downs near Wye
Waymarking	The Countryside Commission acorn symbol. Wooden North Downs Way fingerposts are used extensively in Surrey, whilst in Kent low-level concrete plinths are common
Navigation	Grade B
Maps	O.S. Landranger 1:50 000, Nos 178, 179, 186, 187, 188, 189
	O.S. Pathfinder 1:25 000, Nos TQ: 66/76, 05/15, 25/35, 45/55, 65/75, 85/95, 04/14, 84/94; TR: 05/15, 25/35, 04/14, 24/34, 13/23; SU: 84/94
Alternative routes	There are two alternative routes to Dover from the

small village of Boughton Lees, above the Stour valley to the west of Wye in Kent. The direct line heads south-east to Wye, Stowting, Postling, Etchinghill and the outskirts of Folkestone and then follows the coast to Dover, a distance of 24 miles (38.6 km). The longer route (the so-called Canterbury Loop) aims north-east to visit Chilham and Canterbury before heading south-east to Patrixbourne, Waldershare Park and Dover (32 miles; 51.5 km)

Pilgrims' Way   The Pilgrims' Way is an ancient route from Winchester to Canterbury reputedly used by pilgrims travelling to the shrine of Thomas à Becket. The route generally keeps to the southern slopes of the North Downs and much of it has now been metalled and incorporated into the modern road network. In places the Pilgrims' Way is co-incident with the NDW, which as a National Trail was designed primarily as a scenic walking route avoiding busy roads

Shared LDPs   The NDW and the London Countryway are co-incident for much of the way from the A22 near Gravelly Hill to Hackhurst Downs, west of Dorking, a distance of about 18 miles (29 km). The NDW and the South Coast Way follow the same route from Folkestone to Dover (5 miles; 8 km). The main route of the Saxon Shore Way also follows the route of the NDW from Dover for 4 miles (6.4 km) towards Folkestone. The Downs Alternative of the Saxon Shore Way follows the NDW for a further 6.5 miles (10.5 km) to Tolsford Hill. The NDW and Vanguard Way are common for a few hundred yards in the vicinity of Titsey Woods, south of Farleigh

Other LDPs   The NDW is intersected by the Wealdway near Trottiscliff. The Downs Link starts (or ends) at St Martha's Hill on the NDW. The Wey-South Path starts/finishes at Guildford on the NDW

Transport   Farnham, Dover and Canterbury all have British Rail stations as well as numerous bus services and car parks. There are many other railway stations on or near to the NDW including those at Folkestone, Wye, Maidstone, Otford, Merstham, Dorking and Guildford

Accommodation   There are youth hostels at Canterbury, Kemsing, Crockham Hill, Tanners Hatch and Holmbury St Mary.
B & B accommodation is available in many of the villages and towns on or near the route

Guidebooks

1 *The North Downs Way* by Denis Herbstein (1982), HMSO. 158 pages. The 'official' guidebook containing O.S. 1:25 000 maps with the route of the NDW clearly marked. It is to be replaced in the early 1990s by a new National Trail Guide.

2 *A Guide to the Pilgrims' Way and North Downs Way* by Christopher John Wright (1971; 3rd edition 1981), Constable. 325 pages. Hardback. There is a great deal of historical, architectural and general discussion in this guidebook, but this is unfortunately intermingled with the route description. The Pilgrims' Way from Winchester is also described alongside the notes on the NDW and therefore the route is somewhat difficult to follow in the text. The book includes impractical 1:100 000 black and white maps and is illustrated with a number of black and white photographs.

3 *Discovering the North Downs Way* by David J. Allen and Patrick R. Imrie (2nd edition 1987), Shire Publications. 80 pages. The route is described in detail together with 50 specially drawn maps. The Way has been divided into 25 sections each of about 6 miles (9.6 km) in length. At the start and finish of each section there is access to the route by car and so this guidebook is particularly suitable for those wishing to walk the NDW in short day sections from a home or holiday base. There are details of car parks serving the route and public transport and refreshment possibilities, as well as historical and other information. The Canterbury Loop is included.

4 *Walking on the North and South Downs* by Mark Chapman (1985), Robert Hale. 190 pages. The route of the NDW is described from Dover to Farnham in 11 one-day stages. Each stage begins and ends where public transport and accommodation are available. Circular walks are also described, enabling the walker to return to the point from which the day's walk began having covered a short section of the NDW. Note that the route from Dover to Boughton Lees via Canterbury is omitted. A description of the SDW is also given as well as a 2-day linking route across the western Weald from Farnham via Frensham Little Pond, the Devil's Punchbowl, Haslemere and Rogate to South Harting and the SDW. Sketch maps and black and white photographs are included.

5 *The North Downs Way.* Ramblers' Association Guide. The booklet contains a detailed route

description of the NDW from west to east including the Canterbury Loop. There is also detailed information on public transport and other facilities. Obtainable from Ramblers' Association Kent Area, 11 Thirlmere Road, Barnehurst, Bexleyheath, Kent DA7 6PU.

6   *The North Downs Way.* South-East England Tourist Board Guide. The route is divided into convenient sections and there are details of accommodation. Not a full guide. Available from South-East England Tourist Board (see Useful Addresses).

7   *The Old Road from Canterbury to Winchester* by Hilaire Belloc (1904), Constable. 296 pages. Not a guidebook. Sadly this classic is no longer in print, but a copy may be found in public libraries or second-hand bookshops.

Guided walks

Surrey County Council organise a number of short guided walks throughout the summer months. Some of these include sections of the NDW. Write to Surrey County Council for details (see Useful Addresses). For the Kent section see under Saxon Shore Way

Deviations

Work on the Channel Tunnel, the A20 and the new rail link may necessitate minor changes to this route. However, the route was unaffected by December 1989. The Channel Tunnel Environmental Map will be of use to walkers using the NDW, the Saxon Shore Way and the South Coast Way. This map consists of O.S. maps showing the Shakespeare Cliff workings, the Ashford Inland Clearance Depot and the underground line of the tunnel before it emerges on to the main terminal site. The map shows both closed and proposed footpaths and bridleways in the area. Enquiries to Eurotunnel Exhibition Centre, St Martha's Plain, Cheriton High Street, Folkestone, Kent CT19 4QD. The map can be bought either at the centre (well worth a visit) or by mail order

Description

Although the NDW, like the SDW, traverses chalk downland the two routes are very different in character. The North Downs lack the openness of the South Downs and they are far more wooded. The escarpment is less continuous than that of the South Downs and the line of the NDW does not always keep to the ridge. This leads to a much greater variety of walking than on the South Downs as the NDW traverses open and wooded hillside, heathland, wide river valley, orchard, farmland and finally the chalk cliffs between Folkestone and Dover.

About 120 million years ago a warm, shallow sea covered the area which now forms southern England. Over a vast period of time chalk deposits were laid down in the form of countless seashells. Around 65 million years ago earth movements (those which also thrust up the Alps when the African continent exerted pressure on Europe) created a raised dome structure some 2000–3000 ft (610–915 m) thick topped with chalk and stretching from where the Channel now is to the Thames valley. When the sea receded this great dome was slowly eroded by the elements, exposing clay and sands below the chalk to form the Weald. However, the chalk edges of the dome remain today as the North and South Downs. The modern word *down* comes from the Anglo-Saxon *dun*, meaning a hill.

When the first permanent settlers arrived in the South-East at around 4000 BC the whole of the Weald was covered in impenetrable forest, the Andredsweald. The high chalk ridges provided the only means of travel and prehistoric tracks were later adopted by the Romans and then Christian pilgrims on the way to Thomas à Becket's shrine at Canterbury. It is only in recent history, with the advent of the railways and the modern road system, that the Downs have ceased to be an important means of communication. Fortunately they can still be enjoyed as a means of leisure and as a way of penetrating the true countryside of the South-East.

The NDW commences at the pleasant Georgian town of Farnham in Surrey, the birthplace of William Cobbett, famous for his book *Rural Rides*. The River Wey is soon crossed and then heathland is traversed below the ridge of the Hog's Back to reach the Wey again at the outskirts of Guildford. Here there are the ruins of a Norman castle, several sixteenth- and seventeenth-century houses and a modern cathedral. The Way then climbs to the lonely church on St Martha's Hill at 557 ft (170 m) above the vale of Tillingbourne. At Newlands Corner there is a fine view of Surrey and the Weald, and on a clear day the South Downs at Chanctonbury Ring can be clearly defined. Continuing mainly through woodland the route keeps to the north of the escarpment, passing Netley Heath and Hawkhurst Downs to reach Ranmore Common with its fine St Barnabus's Church, the Church of the North Downs Way. North of here, deep in the woods, is the youth hostel of Tanners Hatch which cannot be reached by motor car. A stay in this hostel is a must for many NDW wayfarers. Here is a rare opportunity to escape much of the twentieth century. There is no electricity and no telephone and the tracks leading to the hostel are often muddy and without lights. Bring a torch. Tanners Hatch youth hostel is situated

The famous stepping stones over the River Mole. When the river is in flood, the footbridge provides an easier alternative a little way upstream

within the Polesden Lacy estate owned by the National Trust. The regency villa is well worth a visit. This fine building is set in beautiful grounds, but unfortunately the house is open only at weekends.

The busy A24 dual carriageway is encountered at the Mole Gap, north of Dorking. Near here is the Burford Bridge Hotel which has several historical associations; John Keats finished *Endymion* here and Nelson bade farewell to Emma, Lady Hamilton from this spot before the Battle of Trafalgar. The River Mole can usually be negotiated by the famous stepping stones, but if in flood the river can be crossed safely by a footbridge a short distance upstream. Box Hill is perhaps one of the most well-known locations in the whole of the South-East and on most days, particularly in mid summer, the place will be thronging with visitors. For all that the hill is a fine viewpoint.

The Downs escarpment is once again followed for several miles, passing Juniper Hill, Colley Hill and the 'temple' on Reigate Hill, before approaching the motorway complex at Merstham. The M25 is crossed by a footbridge and the M23 by an underpass after which there is a stiff pull up Oakley Hill. The line of the M25 is followed for several miles, but mercifully on the escarpment well to the north. There are fine views down to Redhill and Godstone as the Way passes to the north of Oxted and reaches the Surrey/Kent county boundary after Titsey Park, south of Tatsfield.

The path passes through the Chevening estate, the house of which is used by the Foreign Secretary of the day. Soon the Darent valley with Sevenoaks beyond comes into view. The route crosses the London–Sevenoaks railway line and descends to enter suburbia, rejoins the Pilgrims' Way and crosses the River Darent into Otford, a pretty village with green and pond, and steeped in history (Thomas à Becket lived here and Henry VIII stayed in Otford on his way to the Field of the Cloth of Gold). A climb out of Otford leads to the top of the ridge again and this is followed to the north of Kemsing which has a youth hostel. The motorway system is again encountered at Wrotham; this time the M20. The path then follows the ridge of the Downs as it heads towards the north-east to visit the pleasant Trosley Country Park. Nearby is a splendid megalithic burial chamber, Coldrum Long Barrow, owned by the National Trust.

The Medway valley is now approached. A crossing of the marshes and the River Medway was always the great difficulty for pilgrims travelling to Canterbury. Today there is a mile-long motorway bridge crossing the River Medway and the rambler must follow a path alongside this bridge. Once across, the NDW soon climbs back on to the Downs, providing views of the wide sweep of the Medway valley. After Blue Bell Hill the Way passes an interesting neolithic burial chamber at the oddly named Kit's Coty. Maidstone, some 4 miles (6.4 km) to the south, comes into view occasionally and then there is more woodland leading along the ridge and down to Detling. From here the Way crosses farmland at the foot of the Downs before another climb, ridge walk and descent to Hollingbourne.

For many miles now the NDW follows the old route of the Pilgrims' Way, keeping to middle ground away from the crest of the Downs, over Charing Hill and past the picturesque Eastwell Lake and ruined church of St Mary to reach Boughton Lees. The direct route to Dover continues across fields to Wye, an attractive village and home of Wye College, an agricultural establishment and part of the University of London. The route climbs on to Wye Downs, providing marvellous views of the valley. Here is a nature reserve where chalk downland and woodland have been preserved in their virgin state. A feature of the area is the Devil's Kneading Trough, a steep-sided dry valley about 1.5 miles (2.4 km) long. This is downland at its best and it is not surprising that this site was chosen for the opening ceremony of the NDW in 1978.

From Broad Downs the Way continues in a south-easterly direction

Folkestone, seen from the clifftops above Dover. It features in the North Downs Way, the Saxon Shore Way and the South Coast Way

passing near to Stowting and Etchinghill and meeting the Downs Alternative of the Saxon Shore Way. The two LDPs are then co-incident to Folkestone and along the coast to Dover.

The loop of the NDW via Canterbury leaves the direct route at the village of Boughton Lees and passes through Challock Forest to reach the charming, albeit touristy, village of Chilham. The NDW is now deep in the 'garden of England' and there are several miles of orchards before the cathedral and city of Canterbury are reached. Here, of course, there is much of interest for the foot traveller as well as the car tourist. Patrixbourne with its fine Norman church is the first village encountered on leaving Canterbury. The route follows the line of the A2 for a while before pulling away to Shepherdswell and then on to traverse the grounds of Waldershare House, home of the Earl of Guildford. The final miles into Dover are more or less in a straight line heading due south along an old Roman road. A visit to Dover Castle is a fine way to end this scenic and varied journey along the length of the Surrey and Kent Downs.

The white cliffs of Dover, seen on the North Downs Way, the Saxon Shore Way, the Sussex Border Path and the South Coast Way. Note the air shaft for the railway tunnel

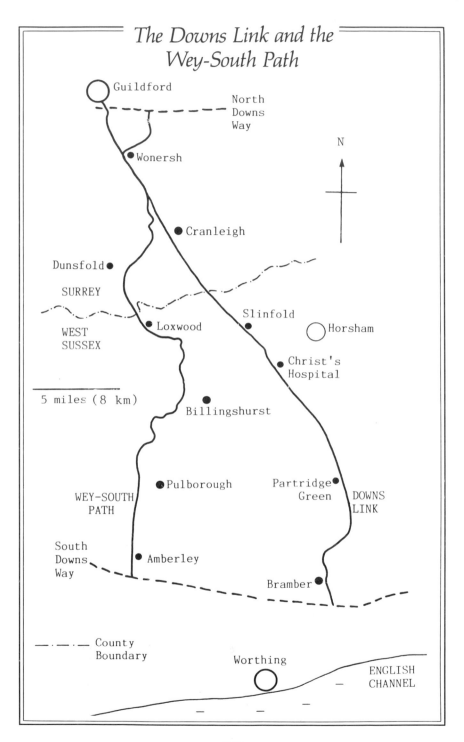

The Downs Link and the Wey-South Path

Guildford

North Downs Way

N

Wonersh

Cranleigh

Dunsfold

SURREY

Slinfold

Loxwood

Horsham

WEST SUSSEX

Christ's Hospital

5 miles (8 km)

Billingshurst

Pulborough

Partridge Green

DOWNS LINK

WEY–SOUTH PATH

South Downs Way

Amberley

Bramber

— · — · — County Boundary

Worthing

ENGLISH CHANNEL

The Downs Link

Information

Length	30 miles (48 km)
Start & finish	St Martha's Hill east of Guildford (Grid ref. TQ 032483) St Botolph's Church, south-east of Steyning (Grid ref. TQ 193094)
Details of route	St Martha's Hill – Bramley – Run Common – Cranleigh – Baynards Station – Rudgwick – Slinfold – Itchingfield – Christ's Hospital – Southwater – Partridge Green – Bramber – St Botolph's Church
Counties traversed	Surrey and West Sussex
Nature of route	A Regional or Recreational Route developed and managed by Surrey and West Sussex County Councils and Waverley Borough Council. The Downs Link is a long distance footpath and bridleway and almost all of the route follows the track of a disused railway line. It can be used by walkers, horseriders and, in some places, cyclists
Average duration	2 days
Landscape	Disused railway. Greensand hills, villages, common and chalk downland
AONBs	The Downs Link passes through part of the Surrey Hills AONB at its northern end and reaches the Sussex Downs AONB at its southern terminus
Date of opening	The official guide to the Downs Link was first published in June 1984. Leaflets on the route first appeared in August 1982 by which time most of the bridleway was negotiable
Waymarking	A special Downs Link symbol (silhouette of a railway arch in green/white) appears on signposts at each end of the trail and at numerous points along the route
Navigation	Grade A. Very easy to follow
Maps	O.S. Landranger 1:50 000, Nos 186, 187, 198 O.S. Pathfinder 1:25 000, Nos TQ: 04/14, 03/13, 02/12, 01/11
Linking LDPs	As its name suggests, the Downs Link joins the NDW at St Martha's Hill in Surrey with the SDW near Steyning in West Sussex
Shared LDPs	The Downs Link is co-incident with the Wey-South Path for about 3 miles (5 km) from Bramley to Run Common south of Guildford

Other LDPs   The Sussex Border Path intersects the Downs Link
                    close to the border between Surrey and West Sussex
                    near Rudgwick. The Greensand Way crosses the
                    Downs Link near Shamley Green
Transport   The nearest British Rail station to the start of the
                    Downs Link is at Chilworth, about 1.5 miles (2.5 km)
                    from St Martha's Hill. There is a railway station at
                    Guildford. At the southern terminus of the path the
                    nearest rail station is at Shoreham-by-Sea, some 5
                    miles (8 km) further south. There is a railway station
                    at Christ's Hospital en route.
                    The services of several bus companies cross the
                    Downs Link and details of routes and times can be
                    obtained from the operators (Alder Valley,
                    Southdown, London Country Bus and Tillingbourne
                    Bus Company – see Useful Addresses). There are
                    several car parks en route and the location of these is
                    indicated on the strip maps in the guide booklet
Accommodation   The nearest youth hostels are at Tanners Hatch,
                    Holmbury St Mary and Truleigh Hill, all some
                    distance from the Downs Link

Guidebooks   1   *Downs Link Route Guide*. This 20-page booklet is
                    the 'official guide' and is available from West Sussex
                    County Council (see Useful Addresses). The guide
                    contains black and white strip maps of O.S. 1:50 000
                    maps with the route of the Downs Link overlaid
                    with a green line. There is a general description of
                    the route together with some historical and
                    topographical information on the villages and sights
                    en route.
                    2   *The South Downs Way and the Downs Link* by Kev
                    Reynolds (1989), Cicerone Press. 136 pages. The
                    route is described in 5 stages in a southbound
                    direction from St Martha's to St Botolph's. There are
                    sketch maps and photographs of the surrounding
                    countryside (see also under SDW guidebooks).
                    3   *A Walk Along the Tracks* by Hunter Davies. First
                    published 1982 (Arrow Paperbacks, 1987). 196
                    pages. Not a guidebook but a well-written account
                    of walks along 10 disused railway lines in Britain.
                    Unfortunately the Downs Link is not included, but
                    another disused track in Sussex (the Worth Way, 6
                    miles (9.7 km), between Three Bridges and East
                    Grinstead) is the subject of one chapter. Good
                    background reading for walking along disused
                    railways.
                    4   *Walking Old Railways* by Christopher Somerville

(1979), David & Charles. 144 pages. Hardback.
Sadly now out of print but can be ordered through
public libraries. Includes a short chapter on the
Shoreham to Christ's Hospital Bridleway.
5   *Railway Walks GWR & SR* by Jeff Vinter (1990),
Alan Sutton. Written by the Chairman of the
Railway Ramblers, this book, the first in a region-by-
region series, contains descriptions of ten branch-line
walks, including the Downs Link. The walks are
broken down into easily walked short sections.
Recommended for all railway walking enthusiasts.

Shorter walks based   Details of short circular walks based on the main
on the Downs Link   route are given in various leaflets available from
West Sussex County Council (see Useful Addresses)

Description

Just after World War II when British Rail came into existence, the railway network consisted of around 19 000 miles (30 577 km) of track
throughout the country. By the early 1980s this had been cut to about
11 000 miles (17 703 km), the majority having been closed after the
publication of the Beeching Report in 1966. Unfortunately, only a few
county councils and local authorities have seized the opportunity to
convert the land liberated after the closure of a railway line into a
worthwhile amenity for the public. The Downs Link is one of the best
and probably the longest recreational path in this country that has been
developed from a disused railway line. The surface, for the most part, is
firm and provides good and easy walking in pleasant surroundings.

The route of the Downs Link follows not one, but three railway lines.
Two of these are now disused and form the majority of the present-day
LDP. The first was the Steyning Line along the Adur valley from
Shoreham to Itchingfield Junction near Horsham. This line, built by the
London Brighton South Coast Railway, had a total of 7 stations
(Shoreham, Bramber, Steyning, Henfield, Partridge Green, West Grinstead and Southwater) and the complete line was opened on 16 Septem-
ber 1861. This was originally a single-track railway, but between 1877
and 1879 it was widened to double track. A second line was also
constructed in the 1860s between Horsham and Guildford. This single
line had 5 stations along its length (Slinfield, Rudgwick, Baynards, Cranleigh, Bramley and Wonersh) and was opened by the Horsham and
Guildford Railway Company on 2 October 1865. These two lines were
separated by a short section of the Pulborough line, which was built at
the same time as the Steyning line, and which is still in use today as the

main line from London via Three Bridges to the south coast at Litt-lehampton.

When the three lines were built it was thought that they would provide a profitable route from the Midlands to the south coast, but they attracted only local traffic and ran at a loss for a long period. In later years the Steyning line was nicknamed the 'linger and die'. It was no surprise that the two lines were amongst the many to close when Beeching's axe fell in the mid-1960s.

The Downs Link descends from St Martha's Hill on the NDW into the Tillingbourne valley, crossing heathland and Wonersh Common to reach the disused railway track north of Bramley, about 3.5 miles (5.6 km) from St Martha's. It then remains on the track for most of its journey south. Much of the clearance work necessary and the refurbishing of the track was carried out by a Manpower Services Commission scheme organised by the various councils.

After Run Common the route reaches Cranleigh where the track must be left for 0.5 miles (0.8 km) as the station site has now been developed. The next station is Baynards which is in private ownership and has been beautifully restored. Shortly after this the railway line went through the 330 yd (301 m) Rudgwick Tunnel, but the entrance of this was filled in shortly after the railway was closed. The route therefore climbs above the tunnel and passes four large oak trees which mark the Surrey/West Sussex County boundary. Shortly after Rudgwick the disused railway crosses over the River Arun on an unusual two-tiered bridge. The route continues past Park Street Nature Reserve and through several cuttings and embankments to reach Slinfold and Itchenfield before meeting the main Horsham railway line (in use) at Christ's Hospital, home of the famous Bluecoat School.

A path alongside the modern railway line soon takes the walker to the old disused track again and this is followed through pleasant Sussex countryside to Southwater and on to Partridge Green and Henfield. Shortly after Stretham Manor (1 mile, (1.6 km) detour to Woods Mill Nature Reserve) the Downs Link leaves the railway track and crosses fields to Bramber Castle. It rejoins the track for the last 0.5 miles (0.8 km) until the SDW crosses it, just to the north of St Botolph's Church.

There are two other disused railway tracks in Sussex which have been converted into long distance walking routes, viz. the Worth Way from Three Bridges to East Grinstead (6 miles; 9.7 km) and the Forest Way from East Grinstead to Ashurst Junction, west of Groombridge (9.5 miles; 15.3 km). Details of these routes can be obtained from West and East Sussex County Councils respectively (see Useful Addresses).

The Wey-South Path

Information

Length	36 miles (58 km)
Start & finish	Guildford (Grid ref. SU 994493)
	SDW south of Amberley (Grid ref. TQ 033123)
Details of route	Guildford – St Catherine's Ferry – Stonebridge – Bramley – Run Common – Elmbridge – Fast Bridge – Three Compasses Inn – Alford – Loxwood – Newpound Common – Newbridge – Stopham Bridge – Hardham – Greatham Bridge – Amberley – SDW
Counties traversed	Surrey and West Sussex
Nature of route	A Recreational route promoted by members of the Wey and Arun Canal Trust. The route uses existing rights of way throughout its length and follows as closely as possible the line of the Wey and Arun Canal which has become largely obliterated
Average duration	2–3 days
Landscape	Downland, greensand hills, woodland, river, canal and marshland
AONBs	The Wey-South Path passes through part of the Surrey Hills AONB and reaches the Sussex Downs AONB on the South Downs
Date of opening	The paths used have always been rights of way. The 'official' guidebook was first produced in 1976
Waymarking	The route has no special waymarks. However, most of the public rights of way used on the route are clearly signposted and waymarked in the usual manner (yellow arrows for footpaths and blue for bridleways)
Navigation	Grade B
Maps	O.S. Landranger 1:50 000, Nos 186, 187, 197
	O.S. Pathfinder 1:25 000, Nos TQ: 04/14, 03/13, 02/12, 01/11
Linking LDPs	The Wey-South Path links the NDW near Guildford with the SDW near Amberley. It is therefore a somewhat longer alternative to the Downs Link (q.v.) which also joins these two National Trails
Shared LDPs	The Wey-South Path is co-incident with the Downs Link for about 3 miles (5 km) from Bramley to Run Common, south of Guildford
Other LDPs	The Sussex Border Path crosses the Wey-South Path at Grid ref. 928325, south-west of Alfold Bars. The

43

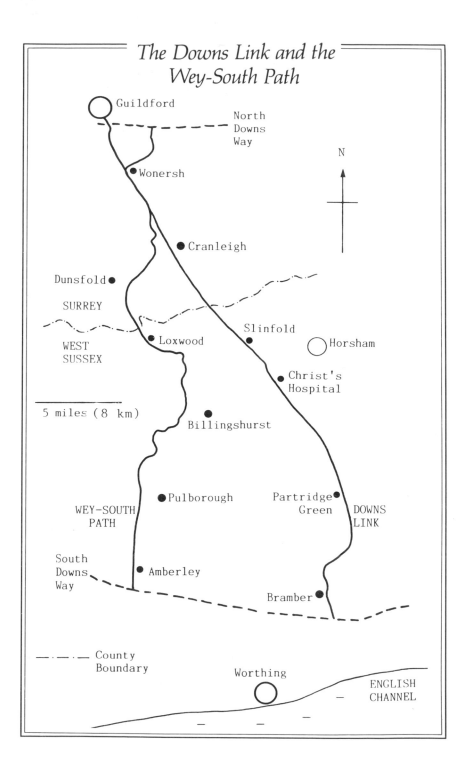

The Downs Link and the Wey-South Path

Guildford

North Downs Way

Wonersh

Cranleigh

Dunsfold

SURREY

WEST SUSSEX

Slinfold

Loxwood

Horsham

Christ's Hospital

5 miles (8 km)

Billingshurst

Pulborough

Partridge Green

WEY-SOUTH PATH

DOWNS LINK

South Downs Way

Amberley

Bramber

N

—.—.— County Boundary

Worthing

ENGLISH CHANNEL

Greensand Way intersects the Wey-South Path near Shamley Green

Transport There is a main-line railway station at the start of the path at Guildford and at its end at Amberley station. Note, however, that Amberley station is closed on Sundays. There is also a railway station at Shalford. Several bus companies operate services in the area. Contact the relevant operators for details (see Useful Addresses).

Car park possibilities are indicated in the guidebook (see below)

Accommodation The nearest youth hostels are at Tanners Hatch, Holmbury St Mary, Truleigh Hill and Arundel, all some distance from the path. Details of hotel and inn accommodation are to be found in the guidebook (see below)

Guidebooks 1 *The Wey-South Path, From Guildford to the South Downs* by Aeneas Mackintosh. This 20-page booklet is produced by the Wey and Aran Canal Trust and is available from their Hon. Sec. at 24 Griffiths Avenue, Lancing, West Sussex BN15 0HW. It contains black and white O.S. 1:50 000 strip maps with the route of the Wey-South Path overlaid with a clear black line. There is a fairly detailed route description together with points of interest on the countryside and the history of the canal. Transport and accommodation details.

2 *London's Lost Route to the Sea. An Historical Account of the Inland Navigation which Linked the Thames to the English Channel* by P.A.L. Vine (first published 1965), David & Charles. 267 pages. Hardback. Not a guidebook but recommended background reading for anyone planning to walk the Wey-South Path. It is a detailed study of the Wey and Arun Junction Canal written for the general reader and illustrated with a number of black and white photographs.

Description

The Wey-South Path is the second of the two LDPs which specifically link the North and South Downs Ways. Whereas the Downs Link takes a disused railway line as the basis of a route, the Wey-South follows the line of a canal, 'London's lost route to the sea'. The Wey and Arun Canal was built to link the River Wey in Surrey with the River Arun in Sussex and so form an inland waterway route from London to the south coast.

The Wey-South Path near Wisborough Green, West Sussex. The path traverses Newpound Common on its way to join the River Arun at Pallingham near Pinkhurst

Henry Fitzalan, the 22nd Earl of Arundel, was responsible for clearing and widening the channel of the Arun down to the sea between 1545 and 1574, thus enabling barges to reach Pallingham Quay above Pulborough. The River Wey was made navigable up to Guildford in 1653 and opened as far as Godalming in 1763. Proposals to link the two rivers by canal date back to 1641, but the system was not finally operational until 1816. The Wey and Arun Canal in fact consisted of two canals; the Arun Navigation, opened in 1787, which brought craft as far as Newbridge, near Billingshurst, and the Wey and Arun Junction Canal, opened in 1816, which completed the link from Newbridge to the River

Wey at Stonebridge, near Shalford. The canal had a short working life, reaching its peak as a commercial waterway in 1839, but rapidly declined after the railway arrived in Sussex. It was the opening of the Horsham to Guildford railway in 1865 that finally sounded the death knell and forced the canal to close in 1868. Ironically the railway was itself to close a century later and form the basis of the Downs Link LDP.

The Wey and Arun Canal is 23 miles (37 km) long, 25 ft (7.6 m) wide and about 4 ft (1.2 m) deep. There were originally 26 locks, but only 10 remain today in various states of decay. There were 35 bridges and numerous wharves, lock houses and aqueducts. Much of the canal remains today although dried up and overgrown and in 1970 the Wey and Arun Canal Society (later a charitable trust) was set up with the objective of restoring the canal as a navigational link for recreational use. Further details about the trust, as well as application forms for membership, can be obtained from the Honorary Secretary (address under Guidebooks, see earlier).

It is possible to start the walk at Weybridge on the Thames and follow the towpath along the River Wey (owned by the National Trust – public access) but the Wey-South Path proper starts in the centre of Guildford. The River Wey is followed past the site of St Catherine's Ferry with its small grotto and stream and soon reaches the Wey and Arun at a short arm of the canal, the only section remaining navigable. The path joins up with the Downs Link route until Run Common and then follows the line of the canal to Fast Bridge (one of the best-preserved bridges on the canal) and the Three Compasses Inn on the edge of Dunsfold Aerodrome. The route always follows right of way and so has to leave and rejoin the towpath at several points along the way. At Rosemary Lane near Alford the canal towpath is followed for 4 miles (6.4 km) past Loxwood. In this region there were 9 closely spaced locks, but these were destroyed in World War II for demolition practice. At Loxwood the canal runs to the back of the Onslow Arms Inn and continues down 8 further locks for another 8.5 miles (13.7 km) to join the River Arun at Pallingham Quay. The Wey-South Path leaves the canal for several miles to pass Newpound Green. Wisborough Green is skirted to the east and the Arun is finally reached at Pallingham near Pinkhurst. The way heads south for a further 5.5 miles (8.9 km) to Amberley and from here climbs on to the Downs to meet the SDW at the top of Mill Lane. Amberley railway station is close by. From here it is quite feasible to follow the river towpath (a right of way) to Arundel and on to Littlehampton, a splendid and straightforward walk. It is therefore quite possible to walk from the Thames to the English Channel or indeed, by making use of the Thames Path (q.v.), from London to the sea.

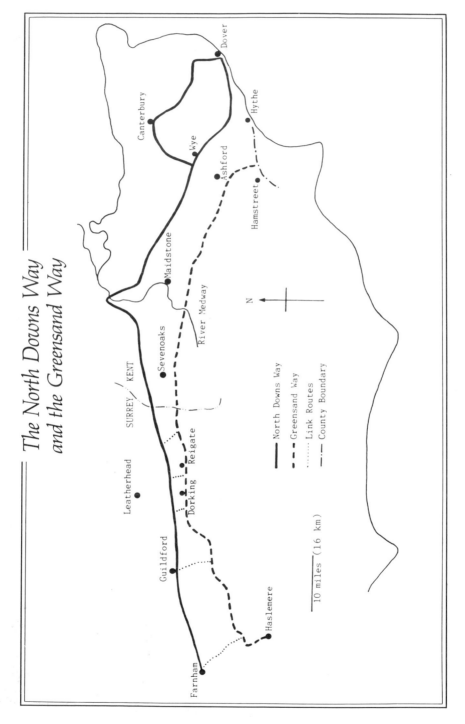

The North Downs Way and the Greensand Way

Dover
Hythe
Canterbury
Wye
Ashford
Hamstreet
Maidstone
River Medway
Sevenoaks
SURREY / KENT
Leatherhead
Reigate
Dorking
Guildford
Haslemere
Farnham

N

——— North Downs Way
– – – Greensand Way
········ Link Routes
–·–·– County Boundary

10 miles (16 km)

The Greensand Way

Information

Length	105 miles (169 km)
	Surrey section: 55 miles (89 km)
	Kent section: 50 miles (80 km)
Start & finish	Haslemere (Grid ref. SU 906330)
	[(Limpsfield High Chart (Grid ref. TQ 437523)]
	Saxon Shore Way near Hamstreet (Grid ref. TR 019349)
Details of route	Haslemere – Hindhead – Thursley – Witley – Hambledon – Hascombe – A281 – Winterfold Hill – Pitch Hill – Holmbury St Mary – Leith Hill – Dorking – Deep Dene – Betchworth – Reigate Park – Earlswood Common – South Nutfield – Bletchingley – Tandridge – Oxted – Limpsfield – French Street – Toys Hill – Ide Hill – Weald Church – One Tree Hill – Ightham Mote – Shipbourne – West Peckham – Yalding – Buston Manor – Linton – Sutton Valence – Ulcome – Liverton Street – Egerton – Pluckley – Hothfield – Great Chart – Stumble Lane – Saxon Shore Way near Hamstreet
Counties traversed	Surrey and Kent
Nature of route	A Regional or Recreational Route. The Surrey section of the Way was originally sponsored by the Surrey Amenity Council (now the Surrey Society) with the active help of the Ramblers' Association and with support from the Countryside Commission and Surrey County Council. In the late 1980s responsibility for the route was assumed by Surrey County Council. The Kent section was conceived and developed by the Kent area of the Ramblers' Association
Average duration	One week
Landscape	Greensand hills, villages, farmland, orchards and hopfields
AONB	The Surrey section of the Greensand Way runs almost exclusively through the Surrey Hills AONB
Date of opening	The middle section of the Surrey Greensand Way, from Winterfold Heath to the Nower, Dorking (12 miles; 19 km), was opened at a Ramblers Rally, to commemorate Footpath Heritage Year, held on 15 June 1980. The remainder of the Surrey section was opened in 1982. The West Kent section from

Limpsfield Chart to Yalding station was opened in April 1986 and the final East Kent section was declared open by Fay Godwin, President of the Ramblers' Association, at a ceremony held in Sutton Valence on Saturday 15 April 1989

Waymarking The route is waymarked with yellow or blue discs bearing the inscription GW. Standard yellow and blue arrows are also used. In Kent the GW waymark is often found on stone plinths indicating a public footpath or bridleway. The line of the route is occasionally indicated with a line of wooden stakes tipped with yellow and bearing a GW mark

Navigation Grade B. Parts of the Kent section are perhaps Grade B/C

Maps O.S. Landranger 1:50 000, Nos 186, 187, 188, 189 O.S. Pathfinder 1:25 000. Surrey section: Nos SU 83/93; TQ: 03/13, 04/14, 24/34, 25/35, 45/55. East Kent section: Nos TW 65/75; TQ: 64/74, 84/94, 85/95, 83/93; TR 03

Shared LDPs The West Kent section of the Greensand Way follows the line of the London Countryway for much of the way between Limpsfield High Chart and Ightham Mote, a distance of about 12 miles (19 km)

Other LDPs The Greensand Way joins the Saxon Shore Way 1.5 miles (2.4 km) from Hamstreet, about 13 miles (20.9 km) north-east of Rye. The Wealdway crosses the Greensand Way at Oxen Hoath (Grid ref. 629524) near West Peckham, and the Vanguard Way intersects on Limpsfield Chart, north of Crockham Hill. The Greensand Way crosses both Downs Link and the Wey-South Path near Shamley Green at a point where the latter two routes are coincident

Link routes There are 5 waymarked routes linking the Greensand Way to the NDW National Trail. These enable sections of both routes to be combined in circular walking tours.
Link 1 Thursley Church (Grid ref. SU 902393) to Moor Park, Farnham (Grid ref. SU 862466). 6.25 miles (10 km). Maps: Landranger 186; Pathfinder SU 84/94.
Link 2 Rooks Hill Farm (Grid ref. TQ 034428) to Guildford (Grid ref. SU 995940). 5 miles (8 km). Maps: Landranger 186; Pathfinder SU 84/94, TQ 04/14.
Link 3 Milton Street, Westcott (Grid ref. TQ

149486) to Ranmore Common car park (Grid ref TQ 142503). 1.75 miles (2.8 km). Maps: Landranger 187; Pathfinder TQ 04/14.
Link 4   Skimmington Castle (Grid ref. TQ 247496) to Reigate Hill (Grid ref. TQ 263524). 3 miles (4.75 km). Maps: Landranger 187; Pathfinder TQ 24/34, TQ 25/35.
Link 5   Oxted Mill (Grid ref. TQ 390518) to Woldingham Road, NDW (Grid ref. TQ 383546). 2.5 miles (3.9 km). Maps: Landranger 187; Pathfinder TQ 25/35.

Transport

There is a British Rail station at the start of the walk at Haslemere. At the end of the route in Kent, Hamstreet railway station is reached by following the Saxon Shore Way for about 1.5 miles (2.4 km) towards the south-west. The end of the Surrey section/start of the Kent section of the Greensand Way is served by a train to Oxted, 3.5 miles (5.6 km) from Limpsfied High Chart. There are also railway stations at Yalding, Sevenoaks, Nutfield, Betchworth and Witley en route

Accommodation

There are youth hostels at Hindhead, Holmbury St Mary and Crockham Hill

Guidebooks

1   *The Greensand Way in Surrey. A Walker's Guide* (1989). Published by Surrey County Council. 47 pages. The route has been divided into 14 stages and is described in both directions. Clear route descriptions with adjacent, well-drawn sketch maps. Grid references are given for the start and finish points of each section. Pen and ink illustrations. The 5 Link Routes are described in detail. Comprehensive public transport information. Well presented and recommended. Available from Surrey County Council (see Useful Addresses).
2   *The Greensand Way Long Distance Footpath, West Kent Section, 20 miles.* Published by the Ramblers' Association Kent Area: 11 Thirlmere Road, Barnehurst, Bexleyheath, Kent DA17 6PU. Five route cards describing the route from Limpsfied High Chart to Yalding railway station in 10 sections. A detailed route description (west to east only) together with clearly drawn sketch maps at 1:25 000. Notes on places of interest are also included. The cards are contained in a plastic wallet.
3   *The Greensand Way Long Distance Footpath, East Kent Section, 30 miles.* Published by the Ramblers' Association and available from the address given for

point 2 above, or from 42 Waldron Drive, Loose, Maidstone, Kent ME15 9TH. Six cards describe the route in 11 sections from Yalding station to the Saxon Shore Way near Hamstreet (route description is from west to east only). The text is accompanied by clearly drawn sketch maps at 1:25 000. Brief notes on places of interest are included and the cards are contained in a card folder and plastic wallet.

Guided walks
Surrey County Council organise guided walks along the Surrey section of the Greensand Way and its Link Routes during the summer months. These are led by Rights of Way officers and other experienced walkers and are normally limited to 30 people. Either part or whole of the Surrey section of the Greensand Way can be walked in this way (the whole route of 55 miles (89 km) is walked over 5 days). Details from Surrey County Council Countryside Section (see Useful Addresses). For the Kent Section see under Saxon Shore Way

Description

Apart from the two major chalk ridges of the North and South Downs, there is a third range of hills in the South-East of England composed of another sedimentary rock, namely greensand. This rock is older than the chalk, having been laid down prior (i.e. below) the chalk but was brought to the surface following the substantial earth movements and subsequent erosion by water that also formed the North and South Down escarpments. The chemical glauconite laid down with the sandstone gives the rock a greenish tinge, hence the term greensand. Two layers of Greensand, Upper and Lower, separated by a layer of gault clay were in fact deposited on a thick bed of wealden clay. It is the Lower Greensand layer that forms the Greensand Ridge, a range of low hills stretching across Kent and westwards into Surrey to the south of the North Downs and roughly parallel with them. Lower Greensand is a relatively hard sandstone being especially resistant to the forces of erosion, which leads to the formation of hills with a distinctive scarp. In Surrey west of Dorking the greensand hills are very apparent and it is here that the highest point in the South-East is to be found, on top of Leith Hill nearly 1000 ft (305 m) above sea level. South of Farnham the Greensand Ridge curves south along the Hampshire border between the North and South Downs, finally petering out near Haslemere.

The Greensand Way, as the name implies, follows the Greensand Ridge for a little over 100 miles (160 km) from Haslemere across Surrey

An orchard in springtime on the Greensand Way in West Kent, part of the 'Garden of England'

and Kent to join the Saxon Shore Way near Hythe. The route, particularly that in West Surrey, links some of the loveliest country in the whole of the South-East, visiting several well-known beauty spots. The project was originally conceived by the late Geoffrey Hollis of the Ramblers' Association. Unfortunately he never lived to see the opening of the final section of the Way through Kent. The very first stretch of the Greensand Way was opened in 1980, but it was not until the end of the decade that the whole route was established.

The Greensand Way begins in the pleasant country town of Haslemere and climbs over Hindhead Common, an unspoilt area of some 1400 acres owned by the National Trust, to Hindhead village, one of the highest in Surrey. A visit is made to Gibbet Hill at 894 ft (273 m), Surrey's second-highest summit and a famous viewpoint. The hill is named after the gibbet that was erected here to despatch three felons who in 1786 robbed and brutally murdered an unknown sailor in the vicinity. Legend has it that the corpses were left to hang for three years until in a fierce thunderstorm the remains were finally blown to the ground. The old Portsmouth road is followed for 2 miles (3.2 km) along the rim of the Devil's Punchbowl, a dramatic, steep-sided amphitheatre covered in deciduous woodland and bracken. The path leads to Thursley churchyard where the grave of the sailor murdered on the Punchbowl will be found.

The route swings east along the southern boundary of Witley Park to Brook and Sandhills and crosses the railway at Witley station. Witley is the usual starting point for the annual Surrey Summits 100 km (62 miles) challenge walk over the hills of central and western Surrey including sections of the Greensand and North Downs ridges. It is organised by the Long Distance Walkers Association (see Useful Addresses). The Greensand Way passes Hambledon Common and follows the line of the Hambledon Hills over Vann Hill, but unfortunately omits Hydon's Ball, 0.5 miles (0.8 km) to the north, where there is a memorial seat to Octavia Hill, co-founder of the National Trust. A climb over Holloways Heath leads to Hascombe and then north to Winkworth Arboretum to descend towards Cranleigh Water, crossing the disused railway track and the old Wey and Arun Canal.

The next 12 miles (19.3 km) are possibly the finest of the whole route. At Shamley Green an ascent to Winterfold Heath leads to the attractive

The church in East Sutton Park between the villages of Sutton Valence and Ulcombe on the Greensand Way in East Kent

Left *The route of the Greensand Way passes the pleasant church of St Nicholas at Boughton Malherbe, deep in rural Kent*

area of Hurtwood, 4000 acres of pine, beech, heather, bracken and bilberries (or hurts) dedicated to the public. These heaths and commons, a maze of sandy tracks, are administered by the Hurtwood Control Committee, a group of lords of the manor. There are many ups and downs as the route leads along the main greensand ridge to Reynard's Hill (800 ft; 244 m), Pitch Hill (843 ft; 257 m) and the memorial seat on the summit of Holmbury Hill (857 ft; 261 m), the site of a large iron age hill fort. The views from these heights are very extensive, across the Weald to the South Downs. After the village of Holmbury St Mary the Greensand Way climbs to the summit of Leith Hill (965 ft; 294 m). The 60 ft (18.3 m) tower (open most weekends and holidays) was built in 1766 by one Richard Hull of nearby Leith Hill Place in order to elevate the hill, albeit artificially, to that of a mountain, i.e. over 1000 ft.

From Leith Hill the way swings to the north for a long descent down the Tillingbourne valley, through the Evelyn Estate, past a small waterfall and a series of trout pools. Before reaching the A25 the route turns back to the east to Milton Street by Bury Hill Lake and on via the Nower

The ruins of St Leonard's Chapel, a short detour from the line of the Greensand Way in Kent

Right *The unusual Bell House, found in the village of Boughton Malherbe in Kent* and Glory Wood to Dorking. Beyond the town the railway and River Mole are crossed as the path continues to Brockham, Betchworth and Reigate Heath with its most unusual windmill church. And so on to Bletchingley and over Tilburstow Hill to the historic village of Tandridge, whose churchyard has a yew tree reputed to be well over 1000 years old. A route to the south of Oxted and Limpsfield (where the grave of Delius may be seen in the churchyard) leads up to the woods of Limpsfield Chart where the county boundary is crossed.

The Way continues into Kent over Crockham Hill Common, passing close to Chartwell, the home of Sir Winston Churchill, one of the National Trust's most visited properties. A traverse of Hosey Common leads to Toys Hill and Ide Hill, both fine viewpoints also owned by the National Trust. The route descends to the Sevenoaks Weald to cross

Greensand Way sign in Coldham Wood, Kent

West Peckham village green. The church in the village has a Saxon tower and is said to have the finest 'squire's pew' in Kent

Knole Park. Knole House, one of the largest private houses in England, now owned by the National Trust, is situated in this elegantly land-scaped deer park. The beautiful old manor house of Ightham Mote is passed en route for Shipbourne and West Peckham, before the Green-sand Ridge is left to cross the Medway flood plain to Yalding, birthplace of the poet Edmund Blunden. There are many fine seventeenth-century houses to be admired at Yalding before climbing back on to the Green-sand Ridge to follow it through the villages of Linton and Sutton Val-ence, where there are fine views south over the Weald of Kent. The Way passes orchards and hopfields and links the attractive villages of Ulcombe, Egerton, Pluckley and Little Chart.

After Little Chart Forstal, where the novelist H.E. Bates lived, the route begins to turn towards the south, traversing Hothfield Common, Godinton Park and Loudon Wood to Great Chart. The Greensand

The roofs of Sutton Valence, a village built on different levels cut out of the hillside. It is dominated by its public school, founded in 1576

Hop fields are a common site on the Kentish landscape. This one is near Sutton Valence on the Greensand Way

Ridge becomes indistinct from here on but the Way continues through an attractive rolling landscape of wood and farmland. South of Kingsnorth the Way passes an interesting pets' cemetery beneath an area of woodland. Here there are many graves containing the remains of a variety of fondly remembered animals, particularly dogs and cats. Some of the headstones are fairly elaborate structures, with the name of the pet inscribed together with an apt verse. After Ruckinge Crossing the Greensand Way soon meets the Saxon Shore Way which the wayfarer can follow to the railway station at Hamstreet.

Left The Greensand Way in East Kent crosses Hothfield Common near Ashford. A wooden footbridge takes the walker across the tranquil River Stour

An oast house at Little Chart Forstal. These attractive buildings, often converted into private residences, are a common site in the Kent countryside

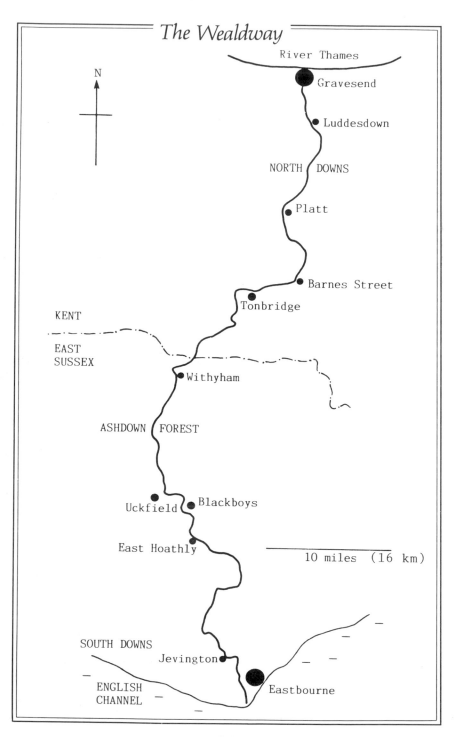

The Wealdway

River Thames

N

Gravesend

Luddesdown

NORTH DOWNS

Platt

Barnes Street

Tonbridge

KENT

EAST
SUSSEX

Withyham

ASHDOWN FOREST

Uckfield

Blackboys

East Hoathly

10 miles (16 km)

SOUTH DOWNS

Jevington

ENGLISH
CHANNEL

Eastbourne

The Wealdway

Information

Length	80–2 miles (129–32 km)
Start & finish	Gravesend (Pier, Grid ref. TQ 647745 or A2, Grid ref. TQ 643712) Eastbourne (Youth Hostel, Grid ref. TV 588991) or Beachy Head (Grid ref. TV 591958) or St Bede's School (Grid ref. TV 60197?)
Details of route	Gravesend – Sole Street – Luddesdown – Great Buckland – Wrotham Heath – Platt – West Peckham – Barnes Street – Tonbridge – Hayesden – Bidborough – Speldhurst – Fordcombe – Withyham – Ashdown Forest – Camp Hill – Five Ash Down – Uckfield – Blackboys – East Hoathly – Chiddingly – Gun Hill – Hellingly – Horsebridge – Arlington – Wilmington – Folkington – Jevington – Eastbourne
Counties traversed	Kent and East Sussex
Nature of route	A Regional or Recreational Path. The route was conceived and developed by members of the Ramblers' Association working as the Wealdway Steering Group. The Way is managed and funded by Kent and East Sussex County Councils
Average duration	6 days
Landscape	Weald, downland, heath, forest, parkland, villages and towns
AONBs & Heritage Coasts	The Wealdway crosses the Kent Downs AONB and finishes on the Sussex Downs AONB. Much of the central section of the walk traverses the High Weald AONB. The route finishes at Beachy Head on the Sussex Heritage Coast
Date of opening	The Wealdway was opened by Sir Derek Barber, Chairman of the Countryside Commission, at a ceremony at Camp Hill in the Ashdown Forest on Sunday 27 September 1981
Waymarking	A distinctive WW symbol carved on wooden posts and stiles
Navigation	Grade B
Maps	O.S. Landranger 1:50 000, Nos 177, 188, 198, 199 O.S. Pathfinder 1:25 000, Nos TQ: 67/77, 66/76, 65/75, 64/74, 44/54, 43/53, 42/52, 41/51, 40/50; TV 49/59/69

Linking LDPs The Wealdway links the Saxon Shore Way and the London Countryway at Gravesend with both the South Downs Way and the South Coast Way at Eastbourne

Shared LDPs The first 5 miles (8 km) of the Wealdway from Gravesend to Sole Street follows the same line as the London Countryway. These two routes are again co-incident between Boughurst Street Farm (south of Great Buckland) and the M20, a distance of nearly 3 miles (4.8 km). The London Countryway rejoins the Wealdway for a few hundred yards south of the A20 before the two routes part for the last time just north of Platt. The Wealdway first meets the SDW at Jevington and later joins it for nearly a mile (1.6 km) on Willingdon Hill near Eastbourne

Other LDPs The Wealdway crosses the NDW and Pilgrim's Way at Trottiscliff and the Sussex Border Path near Groombridge. The Vanguard Way crosses the Wealdway no less than 3 times: north of Camp Hill in the Ashdown Forest, near Blackboys east of Uckfield and finally at Chiddingly. The Wealdway also crosses the Forest Way Country Park (disused railway trackbed – see under Downs Link) north of Withyham

Transport &
Accommodation There are British Rail stations at Gravesend and Eastbourne for the start and finish of the trail. There are also railway stations at Sole Street (5 miles from Gravesend), Tonbridge (28 miles) and Uckfield (54 miles, 0.6 miles off route). There are numerous bus services along the Way.

There are youth hostels at Blackboys (mile 56 from Gravesend) and at Beachy Head at the end of the trail. A detailed accommodation list and a guide to public transport, regularly updated, can be obtained from Keith B. Potter, 11 Thirlmere Road, Barnhurst, Bexleyheath, Kent DA7 6PU

Guidebooks 1 *Wealdway Long Distance Footpath*. The 'official' guidebook produced and published by the Wealdway Steering Group. This 36-page booklet was first published in 1981 and contains first-rate strip maps of the route based on O.S. 1:25 000 maps. The maps are annotated by hand with essential route descriptions and points of interest along the Way. The book is illustrated with attractive pen and ink drawings. It can be ordered separately or together with an up-to-date Wealdway Accommodation and Transport Guide, from

Ramblers' Association National Office or from Keith B. Potter, as above. Recommended.

2 *The Wealdway and the Vanguard Way. A Walker's Guide* by Kev Reynolds (1987), Cicerone Press. 160 pages. The Wealdway is described in six sections, each ending at a place where some form of accommodation is available. The daily stages vary from 9 to 18.5 miles (14.5 to 29.8 km) in length. There is a detailed route description as well as 'things seen on the way' sections for each stage. There are brief details of accommodation and transport possibilities together with the author's personal reflections on the walk. There are a number of black and white photographs. As it is combined with the other major LDP traversing the Weald, the book represents good value for money.

3 *A Guide to the Wealdway* by John N. Mason (1984), Constable. 224 pages. Hardback. Route descriptions from north to south and from south to north are given together with sketch maps (1:50 000) of the route. There are descriptions of places of interest en route as well as suggested diversions. Public transport and accommodation possibilities are outlined and the book is illustrated with black and white photographs.

4 *The Forest — Ashdown in East Sussex* by Barbara Willard (1989), Sweetham Press. 232 pages. Hardback. Not a guidebook but excellent background reading to the Ashdown Forest which is crossed by both the Wealdway and the Vanguard Way. The history of the Forest and the people who have lived there from Roman times to the present day. The book is illustrated with a fine collection of colour photographs

Shorter walks based on the Wealdway	See under Vanguard Way
Guided walks	See under Saxon Shore Way

Description

The Wealdway traverses the Weald of Kent and East Sussex from the Thames at Gravesend to the coast at Eastbourne. In so doing it crosses both the North and the South Downs as well as the Greensand Ridge, the Medway valley and the Ashdown Forest. This is a walk of great variety and interest.

In Roman and later in Saxon times the Weald (from the Saxon *wald* or forest) was covered by an impenetrable forest, the Andredsweald (Anderida to the Romans), the haunt of wild boar, deer and wolves. This great forest was sparsely populated; Andredsweald in the time of the Domesday Book was the 'wood where nobody dwells'. However, the forest was slowly cleared during the fifteenth to eighteenth centuries to exploit the rich iron deposits, to fire furnaces for charcoal and to provide timber for ship and house building. Today there are many small deciduous woods dotted throughout the Weald, the last remnants of the great ancient forest. Several of these are encountered on the Wealdway; in springtime they ring to the sound of birdsong. The Wealden clay is very different from the chalk of the Downs and nowadays there is considerable arable farming in the area; both wheat and grass grow well on this soil.

After an optional 2-mile (3.2 km) road plod up from the pier at Gravesend, the Wealdway enters open countryside to Sole Street where

Plaque celebrating the opening of the Wealdway in 1981 on Camp Hill in the Ashdown Forest

there is an attractive Tudor yeoman's house owned by the National Trust. The path soon reaches Luddesdown and climbs on to chalk downland in the vicinity of the wide sweep of the Bowling Alley, a distinctively shaped valley. In the early 1980s Luddesdown was almost acquired by the military; there was a public outcry and eventually the land was left for the enjoyment of all. The North Downs are descended near Trottiscliff and the Way continues through Wrotham Heath and Meredith Woods, the largest expanse of woodland remaining in Kent. After the pretty village of West Peckham the route passes through hop gardens and orchards dotted with oast houses, to reach and follow the River Medway into Tonbridge, a splendid riverside walk. The Medway is navigable all the way from Tonbridge to the sea at Rochester. The river is encountered further downstream on two other LDPs in the South-East, viz. the NDW and the Saxon Shore Way (q.v.).

Tonbridge is famous both for its public school, founded in 1553, and for the ruins of its Norman castle. There are also several fine old buildings in the town well worth a visit, including the sixteenth-century Chequers Inn a short distance from the castle. The Wealdway passes beneath the castle walls, leaving Tonbridge to follow the Medway along the 'straight mile' before leaving the river to head south through a series of villages and hamlets, Bidborough, Modest Corner, Speldhurst, Bullingstone, Fordcombe and Stone Cross. The Kent/East Sussex border is met near to the Forest Way Country Park, the disused railway track now used as a recreational path.

After Withyham church the Wealdway follows a road through parkland to Fisher's Gate and soon enters Five Hundred Acre Wood. The path through this woodland was dedicated as a right of way in 1970 (a generous gesture by the owner as part of European Conservation Year).The wood will be well known to addicts of A.A. Milne and the Winnie the Pooh/Christopher Robin books. Milne lived in nearby Hartfield and a detour from the Wealdway leads to Pooh Sticks Bridge, restored in the late 1970s. The Wealdway climbs steadily to Greenwood Gate Clump, a stand of pines which marks at 720 ft (220 m) both the highest point in Ashdown Forest and on the Wealdway. The route traverses the Forest and continues south to enter Buxted Park near Uckfield. Here is the Church of St Margaret the Queen and Buxted Place, now an exclusive hotel and restaurant. There are several other footpaths across the Park which, combined with its ornamental lakes and its deer, makes an extended visit well worthwhile.

The Wealdway meanwhile continues to the village of Blackboys and leaves the High Weald to cross rich farmland and pass through the pleasant communities of East Hoathly, Chiddingly and Hellingly (the 'ly' in these village names is pronounced as in 'lie'). After Upper Horsefield the Way reaches Michelham Priory on the River Cuckmere. This ancient building is cared for by the Sussex Archeological Trust and is

The stand of trees known as Camp Hill in the Ashdown Forest. It was here that the Wealdway was officially opened in 1981 by Sir Derek Barber, Chairman of the Countryside Commission

Buxted Park, East Sussex. The Wealdway traverses this most attractive landscaped parkland, home of a herd of roe deer

The Church of St Margaret the Queen. This typical wealden church is located in Buxted Park, some way from the actual village of Buxted. It is passed on the Wealdway

open to the public. From the Priory the route continues to Arlington with its ancient church and modern reservoir.

The final stage of the Wealdway is a crossing of the South Downs to Beachy Head and the English Channel at Eastbourne. After Wilmington, which also has a priory (ruins) the path climbs to the Long Man of Wilmington, one of the largest chalk figures in England and a familiar landmark. It is of considerable antiquity; it has been suggested that it represents Pol, god of the underworld who stands at its gate. After Jevington, a picturesque Downland village, the Wealdway climbs Combe and Willingdon hills on the Downs to finish officially by the youth hostel on the A259 outside Eastbourne. Most walkers will continue to the cliff tops at Beachy Head before descending to the long promenade at the foot of the Downs which can be followed to the centre of Eastbourne and the railway station for home.

The Vanguard Way

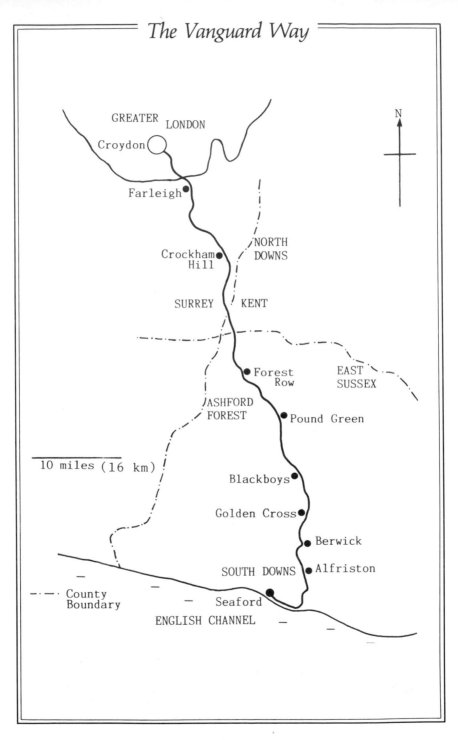

N

GREATER LONDON

Croydon

Farleigh

Crockham Hill

SURREY

KENT

NORTH DOWNS

Forest Row

EAST SUSSEX

ASHFORD FOREST

Pound Green

10 miles (16 km)

Blackboys

Golden Cross

Berwick

SOUTH DOWNS

Alfriston

–·— County Boundary

Seaford

ENGLISH CHANNEL

The Vanguard Way

Information

Length	62 miles (100 km)
Start & finish	East Croydon Railway Station (Grid ref. TQ 328657)
	Seaford Railway Station (Grid ref. TV 482992)
Details of route	East Croydon – Coombe Wood – Selsdon Wood – Farleigh – Chelsham – Botley Hill – Titsey Park – M25 – Limpsfield Chart – Crockham Hill – Edenbridge – Marsh Green – Forest Row – Colemans Hatch – Ashdown Forest – Pound Gate – High Hurstwood – Pound Green – Blackboys – Golden Cross – Berwick Station – Alfriston – Litlington – Exceat – Seaford
Counties traversed	Greater London, Surrey, Kent and East Sussex
Nature of route	A Recreational route devised by the Vanguards Rambling Club linking existing rights of way and freely accessible areas
Average duration	4–5 days
Landscape	London suburbs, parkland, weald, downland, heath, forest, seashore
AONBs & Heritage Coast	The route crosses three Areas of Outstanding Natural Beauty, viz. Kent Downs AONB, High Weald AONB and the Sussex Downs AONB. The trail finishes on Seaford Head opposite the Sussex Heritage Coast
Date of opening	The route was established in 1980 to coincide with the Golden Jubilee of the YHA and the Ramblers' Association's Footpath Heritage '80. The 'official' guidebook was also published in 1980
Waymarking	There are no special Vanguard Way signposts or waymarks along the route. However, the footpaths and bridleways used along the trail are waymarked in the standard manner, i.e. yellow arrows for footpaths and blue arrows for bridleways
Navigation	Grade C
Maps	O.S. Landranger 1:50 000, Nos 187, 188, 199 O.S. Pathfinder 1:25 000, Nos TQ: 26/36, 25/35, 45/55, 44/54, 43/53, 42/52, 41/51, 40/50; TV 49/59/69
Alternative routes	As the Vanguard Way crosses the Wealdway on three occasions it would be quite feasible and interesting to take the Vanguard Way from Croydon

and continue on the Wealdway to Eastbourne. The distance would be approximately 65–70 miles (105–113 km). Alternatively the Wealdway could be followed from Gravesend and the Vanguard Way continued to Seaford (approximately 75–80 miles, 121–9 km)

Shared LDPs

The Vanguard Way shares the route of the SDW from Alfriston to Exceat via Litlington in East Sussex, a distance of about 2.5 miles (4 km). It also follows the NDW for a few hundred yards near Titsey close to the M25. The Vanguard Way can be used as a link route between the two National Trails

Other LDPs

Five other LDPs are crossed as the Vanguard Way threads its way southwards from the suburbs of the capital to the sea. Both the London Countryway and the Greensand Way are crossed on Limpsfield Chart near the Kent/Surrey county boundary. At the Surrey/Sussex border near Dry Hill another LDP is intersected, viz. the Sussex Border Path. At Forest Row the Vanguard Way crosses the Forest Way (disused railway track open to the public). Between the Ashdown Forest and Chiddingly the Vanguard Way and the Wealdway cross each other three times before diverging to make their way to their separate destinations on the south coast

Transport

The path begins and ends at British Rail main line stations, i.e. East Croydon and Seaford. Several other railway stations are on or close to the route, viz. West Croydon, Coombe Road, Woldingham, Oxted (2 miles, 3.2 km off route), Edenbridge, Edenbridge Town, Buxted and Berwick

Accommodation

The Vanguard Way was planned with youth hostels in mind. There are youth hostels at Crockham Hill (mile 15 from East Croydon), Blackboys (mile 41) and Alfriston (mile 56). Using this itinerary the gap between Crockham Hill and Blackboys can be bridged at Forest Row where there are two hotels and B & B accommodation. Details of youth hostels, hotel, B & B, pub and campsite accommodation are given in the 'official' guide (see below)

Guidebooks

1   *The Vanguard Way, A Long Distance Walk from Croydon to the Coast*, written and published by the Vanguards Rambling Club (1980). 48 pages. Available from Ramblers' Association National Office (see Useful Addresses). This is the original guidebook to the route. It contains a very detailed route description together with strip maps at

1:100 000 scale. There are notes on points of interest, black and white photographs and a comprehensive transport and accommodation guide. 2 *The Wealdway and the Vanguard Way – A Walker's Guide* by Kev Reynolds (1987), Cicerone Press. The Vanguard Way is described in 5 sections varying in length from 6 to 15 miles (9.7 to 24 km), each daily section ending at a village where accommodation is available. There are sketch maps, black and white photographs and details of things to see along the route. As the title indicates, the Vanguard Way is combined with the other major LDPs across the Weald and so the book represents good value for money.

Shorter walks based on the Vanguard Way As the Vanguard Way crosses the Wealdway at three places in East Sussex it is possible to devise three circular day walks making use of these two LDPs

Description

The Vanguard Way, a 62-mile (100 km) walk from the London suburbs to the sea, is less well known than the Wealdway but it is essentially the same type of walk and deserves to be more popular. The Vanguard Way and the Wealdway have much in common. They both start in urban surroundings, cross the North Downs and the Greensand Ridge, enter the Weald, traverse Ashdown Forest and cross the South Downs to finish on the chalk cliffs of the south coast. Although they do not start and finish on the North and South Downs (with the exception of the Wealdway which finishes at Eastbourne) the Vanguard Way and the Wealdway can, like the Downs Link and the Wey-South Path to the west, be used to link the North and South Downs in an extended journey.

The walk starts in the most unlikely of places; East Croydon railway station. However, walkers will no doubt be surprised to discover how sylvan Greater London can be. The noise and bustle of the town are soon exchanged for the quiet of parks and woods. The route through Lloyd Park, Coombe and Littleheath Woods leads to Selsdon Woods Nature Reserve (National Trust), 200 acres of woodland administered by the Parks Department of the London Borough of Croydon.

Just before Farleigh the route finally leaves the suburbs of Greater London and continues south past Chelsham and Woldingham to reach the top of the North Downs escarpment on Oxted Downs. A descent by Titsey Park leads to a bridge over the M25. The Vanguard Way crosses Limpsfield Chart and Treveraux Hill and continues to Crockham

Hill for the youth hostel (an alternative route avoids the latter if not required). After Troy Town the River Eden is reached at Haxted Mill, a watermill which dates back to 1680 and which is now a splendid Watermill Museum housing an exhibition of the Wealden Iron Industry. Orchards lead to the highlight of this section, the iron age Dry Hill Fort from where there is a magnificent view over the surrounding countryside. The Way continues south through woodland to reach the small town of Forest Row on the edge of Ashdown Forest.

From around 150 million years ago for a period of many millions of years, a series of sedimentary deposits was laid down in the area that is now the South-East of England, first under a large freshwater lake and later under a warm shallow sea. The first deposit laid down under freshwater conditions was that of Ashdown Sand. This was covered by an alternating series of sands and clays culminating in a thick layer of chalk. Around 65 million years ago substantial earth movements led to the formation of a giant dome, the top of which was located in what is now the centre of the High Weald. Subsequent erosion uncovered the underlying Ashdown Sand at the top of the dome and this elevated area now forms the Ashdown Forest. Ashdown is a royal forest with a recorded history dating back to the thirteenth century. Writing in 1822 William Cobbett described it as 'the most villainously ugly spot' he had ever seen in England. Opinions change and today it is viewed as an area of largely unspoilt beauty and is much frequented by walkers and horseriders. The 6400-acre forest, the largest single piece of open land in South-East England, was purchased by East Sussex County Council in 1989. Its future as a unique area for the enjoyment of the general public is therefore assured. It will continue to be administered by a Board of Conservators who have done so since 1885. The Forest occupies high ground and has more the character of acid heathland than forest, with wide expanses of heather, gorse and bracken, and scatterings of pine. A feature of the area is the number of isolated stands of pine known as clumps which were probably used by hunting parties to lie in wait for deer. Several of these are passed on both the Vanguard Way and the Wealdway. The whole area is criss-crossed with footpaths and rides and if time is available a thorough exploration of the Forest is recommended.

After Forest Row the Vanguard Way climbs on to Ashdown Forest, passing to the south of Coleman's Hatch, crossing the Splash at Newbridge and climbing to the Trig point on Gill's Lap, one of the highest points in the Forest. The route skirts Kings Standing Clump (named after Edward II) and eventually leaves the Forest near Pound Gate. Continuing south the Way now wanders through woodland and across farming country to High Hurstwood, Pound Green and Blackboys. The latter village acquired its name both from a fifteenth-century local squire, Richard Blackboy, and from the local charcoal burners or 'black boys'.

On to Chiddingly with its thirteenth-century church, one of the few in Sussex built of stone. The Way skirts Golden Cross, Chalvington and Arlington Reservoir, built in 1971, to Berwick railway station and on to the church of St Michael and All Angels at Berwick. This occupies a fine viewpoint, having been built on a pre-Christian barrow. There are several modern murals painted by local artists Duncan Grant and Quentin Bell. A path from here leads into Alfriston on the SDW.

From Alfriston the Way crosses the River Cuckmere to Litlington and passes the eleventh-century Charleston Manor to enter Friston Forest, 2000 acres of mainly broadleaved woodland. The SDW is followed to the pond in the picturesque village of West Dean and the famous 227 Steps are climbed to reveal a panorama of the winding oxbows of the Cuckmere. The Seven Sisters Country Park is passed and the Cuckmere River re-crossed at Exceat Bridge as the route heads for Cuckmere Haven and Seaford Head Nature Reserve. From here there are outstanding views of the Seven Sisters chalk cliffs. After an ascent to the Trig point on Seaford Head the Vanguard Way descends to the coastal town of Seaford opposite Newhaven harbour.

Typical scenery of the Ashdown Forest, through which run the Wealdway and the Vanguard Way

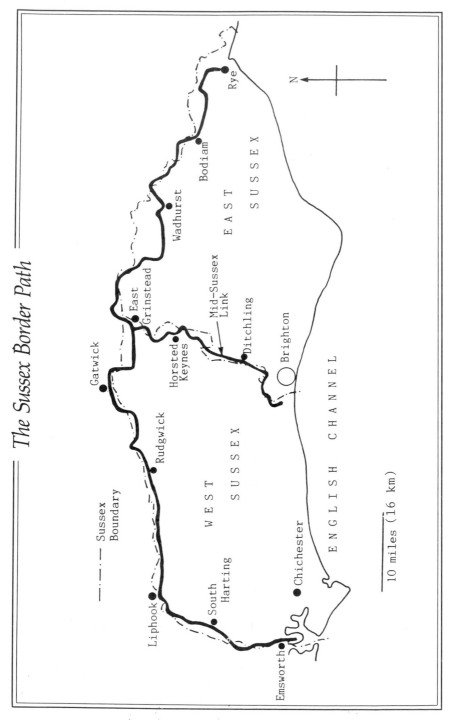

The Sussex Border Path

78

The Sussex Border Path

Information

Length	Main route: 150 miles (242 km) Mid-Sussex Link: 37 miles (60 km)
Start & finish	Emsworth (Royal Oak Public House, Grid ref. SU 753058) Rye (Railway Station, Grid ref. TQ 918205) Mid-Sussex Link: East Grinstead (Railway Station, Grid ref. TQ 388382) Mile Oak, Southwick (Grid ref. TQ 250065)
Details of route	Emsworth – Circuit of Thorney Island – South Harting – Liphook – Gospel Green – Rudgwick – Rusper – Gatwick – East Grinstead – Cowden – Boarshead – Wadhurst – Union Street – Bodiam – Rye. Mid-Sussex Link: East Grinstead – West Hoathly – Horsted Keynes – Scaynes Hill – Ditchling Common – Ditchling – South Downs – Patcham – Mile Oak, Southwick
Counties traversed	West and East Sussex, and also part of Hampshire, Surrey and Kent
Nature of route	A Recreational route linking public rights of way and following as closely as possible the border of the old county of Sussex. The Mid-Sussex Link follows the administrative boundary between East and West Sussex
Average duration	12–15 days. (Mid-Sussex Link: 3 days)
Landscape	Coastline, downland, farmland, woodland, reservoir, river bank
AONBs	The route starts with a 9-mile (14.5 km) walk around Thorney Island peninsula in Chichester Harbour AONB. The western section of the Sussex Border Path passes through East Hampshire and Sussex Downs AONBs whilst most of the eastern half is within the High Weald AONB
Date of opening	The first guidebook to the route was published in 1980
Waymarking	The footpaths and bridleways used on the route are waymarked with standard yellow and blue arrows. Wooden signposts are more common in the western half of the path, whereas low-level concrete plinths

predominate in the eastern section. A number of Sussex Border Path signposts bearing the symbol of a bird were erected along the route in 1989

Navigation   Grade C. Certain sections can be somewhat tricky to negotiate but the Sussex Rights of Way Group has made improvements to the route over the years and so the path is easier to follow than it was when first advocated

Maps   O.S. Landranger 1:50 000, Nos 186, 187, 188, 189, 197, 198, 199

O.S. Pathfinder: SU; 60/70, 61/71, 62/72, 83/93; TQ: 03/13, 23/33, 43/53, 44/54, 63/73, 62/72, 82/92

Alternative routes   By making use of the Mid-Sussex Link it is possible to walk the border of West Sussex from Emsworth to Mile Oak, Southwick and also the border of the East Sussex from Mile Oak to Rye. The original guidebook produced in 1980 included a supplement describing a 36-mile (58 km) route from Rye to Eastbourne following a mainly inland route via Westfield, Battle, Boreham Street and Pevensey, i.e. an alternative to the South Coast Way (q.v.). In the mid-1980s this route was difficult to follow in places, but improvements in the rights of way network may have alleviated the situation

Linking LDPs   The Sussex Border Path links the Wayfarer's Walk and

the Solent Way at Emsworth with the Saxon Shore Way at Rye

Shared LDPs   The last 3 miles (4.8 km) of the Sussex Border Path along the River Rother into Rye are shared with the Saxon Shore Way. The Mid-Sussex Link follows the SDW for about 1 mile (1.6 km) in the vicinity of Devil's Dyke

Other LDPs   By following the borders between Sussex and Hampshire, Surrey and Kent, the Sussex Border Path intersects most of the other LDPs in the South-East. From west to east it crosses the SDW near South Harting, the Lipchis Way (a 26-mile (41.8 km) route from Liphook to Chichester; details from 21 Chestnut Close, Liphook GU30 7JA) south of Liphook, the Wey-South Path south-west of Alfold Bars and the Downs Link near Rudgwick. The Sussex Border Path meets the Worth and Forest Ways (disused railway tracks; send to West and East Sussex County Councils respectively for details – see Useful Addresses) at East Grinstead. It intersects the Vanguard Way near Dry Hill and the Wealdway near Groombridge before finishing at Rye which is also on the South Coast Way

Transport The two termini of the path (Emsworth and Rye) have British Rail stations. There are also railway stations on or near the route at Rowlands Castle, Petersfield, Liphook, Gatwick Airport, East Grinstead, Ashurst and Wadhurst. The Mid-Sussex Link finishes near Southwick where there is a British Rail station. There are numerous bus services covering the countryside through which the Sussex Border Path passes

Accommodation Unfortunately there are no youth hostels close to the route of the Sussex Border Path. The Mid-Sussex Link finishes a few miles from Brighton where there is a youth hostel at Patcham. Hotel and B & B accommodation can be sought at several of the larger villages and towns on or near to the path

Guidebooks 1   *The Sussex Border Path. A Guide to a Long Distance Walk Around Sussex, with detailed strip maps and route description* by Ben Perkins and Aeneas Mackintosh (1984). This 'map pack' consists of a set of 9 route cards contained within a cardboard wallet. The mapping at 1:50 000 is accurate and is based on Ordnance Survey maps. These sketch maps are essential if the path is to be followed without undue problems. The Mid-Sussex Link is included. There are details of public transport services in the vicinity of the path. The guide can be obtained from Ben Perkins at 11 Old London Road, Patcham, Brighton, Sussex BN1 8XR.
2   *The Sussex Border Path* by Aeneas Mackintosh and Ben Perkins (1980). A 47-page booklet containing detailed route descriptions but no maps. The main route is divided into 14 stages ranging from 7.75 to 13 miles (12.5 to 20.9 km) in length. The Mid-Sussex Link is divided into 3 stages (11 to 13 miles; 7.7 to 20.9 km long). An additional 36-mile (58 km) route from Rye to Eastbourne is also included. Enquiries to Ben Perkins at the above address.

Deviations The building of a second terminal at Gatwick has led to a considerable re-routing of the path in the vicinity of the airport

Description

The Sussex Border Path is unique. No other county in England and Wales has a described LDP around its boundary. However, there is no doubt that many other counties could be encircled in this way by using the public rights of way network. For example, John Merrill in 1976 walked the 280 miles (450 km) around the county boundary of Derbyshire using public footpaths and bridleways on or very close to the border. The Sussex Border Path is the work of two ramblers who conceived the idea, planned and walked the route and published a detailed route description and accurate sketch maps (see Guidebooks above). It is a fine example of the work of a few private individuals making use of the existing rights of way network to develop long distance walking routes in the country.

For a county that is never more than 31 miles (50 km) from northern boundary to southern coast, and often considerably less, the length of the Sussex Border Path is perhaps surprising at 150 miles (242 km). If the Mid-Sussex Link between East and West Sussex is included then the route provides almost 190 miles (306 km) of path.

The route commences at Emsworth on the Hampshire border, but before heading north along the boundary the path makes a 9-mile

Sussex Border Path sign near Rowlands Castle

(14.5 km) circuit of Thorney Island. This is actually a peninsula jutting out into Chichester Harbour, the tip of which is the furthest point south-west in Sussex. Thorney Island is free of commercial develop-ment as a result of its being used as an RAF base between 1938 and 1976. However, there is a public footpath around the entire perimeter of the peninsula and this provides remote walking with superb views over the Heritage Coast of Chichester Harbour, the home of a vast number of wildfowl and other birds.

After returning to Emsworth the Sussex Border Path starts out across the coastal plain through wooded and agricultural land to Rowland's Castle. An ascent of Charlton Down, an outlier of the main South Downs ridge, provides extensive views of rolling countryside, after which there is a slow climb through the forest of West Harting Down to cross the line of the South Downs Way. Hemner Hill is descended to South Harting, the largest and most attractive of the three Harting villages. It was the site of a bloody skirmish between Royalists and Parliamentarians in 1643.

The next section is a complete contrast. The first few miles are across the wide flat valley of the River Rother and then the route gently climbs on sandy ground through woodlands and along the foot of Rake Hanger. The border begins to turn to the north-east as sandy tracks are followed to Liphook and across the heathland of Linchmere and Marley Common, wooded areas to the south of Haslemere. West Sussex no longer has Hampshire as a neighbour, but is now bordering on Surrey. One of the highlights of the Border Path is a crossing of Blackdown, with a detour to a superb viewpoint out over the Weald towards the South Downs. Blackdown at 919 ft (280 m) is the highest point in West Sussex. After Gospel Green, the path follows a low ridge, an ancient boundary bank dropping away on both sides of the border, providing good views to both north and south. The county boundary is followed closely for several miles through Rudgwick to the A29 south of Ockley. Careful navigation is required to negotiate a mixture of field and wood-land paths to Rusper and on to Charlwood, once a centre for ironworks but now purely agricultural.

Charlwood is close to the western boundary of Gatwick Airport and the next section is perhaps the least attractive of the entire route. The expansion of Gatwick Airport in the late 1980s greatly disturbed the surrounding area, but it has now been re-landscaped. If somewhat unap-pealing and noisy the area does not lack interest. Fortunately the con-crete of Gatwick is soon left behind. Burstow is a pleasant village; John Flamsteed, the first Astronomer Royal, was rector there for 35 years and the church has several features of interest. A track continues through Copthorne Common amidst fine deciduous woodland to Rowfant, from where a disused landscaped railway, the Worth Way, is taken to East

The famous Mermaid Hotel at Rye, East Sussex. It is passed on the Saxon Shore Way, the Sussex Border Path and the South Coast Way

Rye Church, East Sussex. It houses what is probably the oldest working church clock in England: made in 1562, the clock still possesses its original working parts

Grinstead. From here the Sussex Border Path can be followed along the Kent/East Sussex border, or alternatively the Mid-Sussex Link can be taken south along the West Sussex/East Sussex boundary.

From East Grinstead the Kent/Sussex county boundary follows the ancient Kent Ditch and, as there is no footpath along it, the Sussex Border Path deviates to the north to pass Dry Hill with fine views northwards over the Eden valley to the North Downs. From the attractive village of Cowden the way follows the Kent Ditch closely and the River Medway into Ashurst. It then climbs again through an area of sandstone outcrops, much frequented by rock climbers. Nearing Groombridge it passes close to Harrison's Rocks, the most celebrated climbing ground in the South-East. A few miles further it reaches Bowles Rocks and Outdoor Centre where Julie Tullis, the Himalayan mountaineer tragically killed on K2 in 1986, worked as a climbing instructor. The route then crosses a series of undulating hills and valleys, country typical of the High Weald, passing to the north of Saxonbury Hill and close to Nap Wood, a nature reserve owned by the Sussex Trust for Nature Conservation.

After Wadhurst and Cousley Wood, the Border Path follows the northern perimeter path of Bewl Bridge Reservoir for several miles. This reservoir, constructed in the 1970s, is the largest inland water expanse in the South-East. Fishing and sailing are the main activities. The perimeter path has been tastefully landscaped, passes a reservoir visitor centre and crosses the wide dam. More High Wealden country leads to Bodiam Castle in the valley of the River Rother, one of the finest examples of a medieval moated castle in England. The route continues to Ewhurst Green and the attractive village of Northiam after which some tricky navigating leads to the River Rother which is followed for the last 7 miles (11.3 km) into Rye, a medieval town with cobbled streets and several fine Georgian houses.

The Mid-Sussex Link leaves East Grinstead on the trackbed of the old railway (now known as the Forest Way) which went to Tunbridge Wells. The edge of the large Weirwood Reservoir is followed after which a mixture of field and woodland path crosses unspoilt and often remote country on either side of the Ouse valley to Sharpthorne, Horsted Keynes (for the Bluebell Line steam railway) and Scaynes Hill. After Wivelsfield the path crosses the open Ditchling Common and continues to the village of Ditchling, home of several celebrities from the theatrical world. From this picturesque village the way climbs over the South Downs to Patcham on the outskirts of Brighton. More downland to the hamlet of Saddlescombe and then on to the Devil's Dyke and Southwick Hill to finish at Mile Oak, a short distance from the sea. It was from Southwick that Charles II sailed on his flight to France after his defeat at the Battle of Worcester in 1651.

The Saxon Shore Way

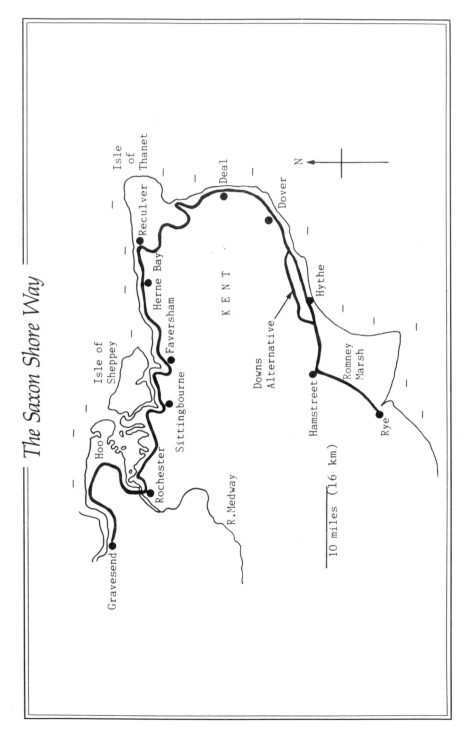

The Saxon Shore Way

Information

Length	140 miles (225 km)
Start & finish	Gravesend (Grid. ref. TQ 646740)
	Rye (Grid ref. TQ 918205)
Details of route	Gravesend – Cooling – Strood – Rochester – Chatham – Lower Halstow – Kingsferry – Sittingbourne – Conyer – Oare – Faversham – Seasalter – Whitstable – Herne Bay – Reculver – Groveferry – Sandwich – Deal – Dover – Folkestone – Sandgate – Hythe – Hamstreet – Appledore – Stone in Oxney – Rye
Counties traversed	Kent (and a very short distance in East Sussex at the end of the walk into Rye)
Nature of route	A Recreational or Regional Path. It was developed by the Kent Rights of Way Council, now no longer in existence, with support from Kent County Council and various district councils and with assistance from the Countryside Commission. The Saxon Shore Way is funded and managed by Kent County Council.
Average duration	9–12 days
Landscape	Thames and Medway estuaries, marshes and creeks, coastline and seaside resorts. Castles, Royal Military Canal, Channel ports, white cliffs and downland.
AONBs & Heritage Coasts	The Way passes through a section of the Kent Downs AONB to the north of Folkestone. The Saxon Shore Way follows the entire length of both the South Foreland Heritage Coast and the Dover–Folkestone Heritage Coast, a total of 8 miles (13 km)
Date of opening	The first guidebook to the route was published in 1980
Waymarking	A distinctive horned helmet, often in red. This occurs on special stone plinths found along the Way. The route is also waymarked with red arrows on a yellow background. This waymarking is absent on the short section which doubles as the NDW
Navigation	Grade B
Maps	O.S. Landranger 1:50 000, Nos 178, 179, 189
	O.S. Pathfinder 1:25 000, Nos TQ: 67/77, 66/76, 86/96, 81/91; TR: 06/16, 26/36, 25/35, 24/34, 13/23, 03, 01/02

Alternative routes Near Folkestone the Way divides. The Shore Route (10 miles; 16.1 km) passes Folkestone Harbour and follows the sea front to Sandgate after which it joins the Royal Military Canal to Hythe and beyond. The Downs Route (13 miles; 20.9 km) climbs inland to join the NDW above the coastal towns. The two routes rejoin on the Royal Military Canal west of Hythe

Linking LDPs The Saxon Shore Way links both the Wealdway and the London Countryway at Gravesend with the Sussex Border Path at Rye

Shared LDPs The Saxon Shore Way follows the NDW for about 6 miles (9.7 km) between Dover and Folkestone. The Downs Path alternative to the Saxon Shore Way follows the NDW for a further 6.5 miles (10.5 km) from Folkestone to Tolsford Hill near Etchinghill. The South Coast Way follows the line of the Saxon Shore Way for about 12 miles (19 km) between Dover and Hythe

Transport The public transport facilities along the Saxon Shore Way are excellent. There are British Rail stations at Gravesend, Strood, Rochester, Chatham, Gillingham, Swale Halt (Kingsferry), Sittingbourne, Faversham, Whitstable, Herne Bay, Sandwich, Deal, Dover, Folkestone, Sandgate (Folkestone West), Sandling, Hamstreet, Appledore and Rye. It is therefore quite easy on this LDP to walk day stages and return to the day's starting point by train. The whole route can be walked in this way. There are also numerous bus services operating from the towns along the route

Accommodation The only youth hostel on the route is at Dover. There is plenty of B & B and hotel accommodation available in the seaside resorts and coastal towns passed en route

Guidebooks 1 *The Saxon Shore Way Guide.* The original set of route cards prepared by the Kent Rights of Way Council is now out of print. The guide has been updated with redrawn maps and route descriptions by the Kent Area of the Ramblers' Association with assistance from Kent County Council. The walk has been divided into 10 stages and at the time of writing only the route cards for stages 1–5 are available (Stage 1: Gravesend to Strood, Stage 2: Medway Towns, Stage 3: Gillingham to Sheppey, Stage 4: Sheppey to Faversham, Stage 5: Faversham to Herne Bay). The guides include notes on places of interest and details of parking and refreshments en route. They can be purchased separately or together. The guides to the remaining stages will eventually become available. Enquiries to Keith B. Potter, 11 Thirlmere Road, Barnhurst, Bexleyheath, Kent DA7 6PU.

2   *The Saxon Shore Way From Gravesend to Rye* by Alan Sillitoe and Fay Godwin (1983). Hutchinson. 192 pages. Recommended. Unfortunately this book is now out of print but a copy may be ordered from a public library. Not a guidebook but an account of Alan Sillitoe's walk along the Way. The text by the well-known author Alan Sillitoe and the black and white photographs by Fay Godwin (professional landscape photographer and past President of the Ramblers' Association) are of a high standard. The book also contains strip maps reproduced from the original guidebook by the Kent Rights of Way Council.

Shorter walks based on the Saxon Shore Way

A publication entitled 'Saxon Shore Walks 1–4, Medway Towns Area' is available from Keith B. Potter (address given above)

Guided walks

Kent County Council operate an extensive programme of short guided walks over the entire county. Some of these often include sections of the LDPs in Kent

Deviations

Work on the Channel Tunnel and the new rail link may necessitate minor changes to this route in the future (see also under NDW – Deviations)

Description

The Saxon Shore Way traces the ancient coastline of Kent. For much of its length this corresponds to the present-day shoreline, the major difference being the Isle of Thanet, which until medieval times was separated from the rest of Kent by a shallow navigable seaway. Hence the LDP thankfully avoids the urban sprawl of Margate, Broadstairs and Ramsgate. The path is named after the Saxon Shore Forts which were built by the Romans in defence against Saxon pirates; four of these are passed en route.

The Saxon Shore Way, particularly the first half from Gravesend to Whitstable, is most unlike any other LDP in the country. At first sight it may seem a very unlikely setting for a pedestrian route, but with perseverance the walker will be rewarded in the exploration of a land unknown to many people. It is a walk of great variety, being in part coastal, rural, urban and industrial. There are strong historical, military

The Royal Military Canal known to walkers of the Saxon Shore Way and the South Coast Way

and literary associations. The surroundings of the first half of the walk are not those usually associated with a walk in the country: saltings, marshes, drainage ditches, creeks, lagoons, brick works, wharves, warehouses and sewage farms abound. But the walker should not be dissuaded by these. There is also a strange atmosphere of loneliness and tranquillity which is captured so evocatively in the photographs of Fay Godwin (see Guidebooks above).

From Gravesend the Saxon Shore Way follows the Thames river wall past Shornemead and Cliffe Forts (nineteenth-century gun-forts) and then makes a circuit of the Hoo peninsula. Cooling Castle and Church (the setting for the opening chapters of Dickens's *Great Expectations*) are passed en route for the Medway bank. This is followed past Upnor Castle (an Elizabethan gun-castle) to Rochester with its fine cathedral and castle. The Medway Towns of Chatham and Gillingham follow, both with strong historical and naval associations, after which the Medway Marshes are crossed by a series of sea walls and creeks over reclaimed marshland. Opposite Chetney, out in Stangate Creek in the Medway Marshes, passenger ships from abroad were often quarantined in the eighteenth century for fear of bubonic plague. At Kingsferry Bridge, one of the historic crossing places of the Swale to the Isle of Sheppey, the route takes Milton Creek inland to Sittingbourne, passing several paper mills (an important industry in north Kent) and follows the two miles of the Sittingbourne and Kemsey Light Railway.

The Way passes an interesting barge museum and returns to the sea wall to follow the Swale for several miles. The industrial past is much in evidence with paper mills, breakers' yards and cement works, but there are also long stretches of sea wall, wetland nature reserves and saltings rich in wildlife. The boatyard and brick works of Conyer lead on to Faversham, the birthplace of gunpowder making in Britain. The remains of the old explosives works are passed en route. There are several scattered workshops, each built out of blast range from the next.

The Saxon Shore Way leaves Faversham via Abbey Street, one of the best preserved streets of seventeenth and eighteenth-century houses in England, and follows Faversham Creek and the Swale over Nagden and Cleve Marshes along the South Swale Nature Reserve. This is the 'oyster coast' which has been famous since Roman times for shellfish. They provided the main industry in the area for hundreds of years but sadly, although cockles and mussels are still plentiful, oysters are now scarce and often contaminated. Pollution and over-fishing are largely to blame. After remote sea walls the route follows the sea fronts of the genteel resorts of Seasalter, Whitstable and Herne Bay.

The ruined Saxon church of Reculver, with its twin towers which are such prominent landmarks to both walkers and mariners, is all that remains of the village of Reculver, built on the site of the Roman fort of

The tow path along such sections of the Royal Military Canal as this one near Hythe in Kent makes for easy, pleasant walking

Regulbium. The sea is still wearing away this coastline at an alarming rate. It is here that the Saxon Shore Way abandons the modern shoreline and crosses the extensive marshlands of the Wantsum Channel. Up until the Middle Ages this was a navigable seaway, forming part of the inshore route from Dover to London. The seaway eventually silted up and the land was drained and reclaimed. After Groveferry the River Stour is followed for several miles towards the giant cooling towers of Richborough Power Station. This was built to take advantage of the river water and the nearby Kent coalfields, on the site of a Roman fort which guarded the southern entrance of the straits which divided the Isle of Thanet from the mainland. The route continues through Sandwich, the first of the Cinque Ports met en route, crosses the internationally famous Royal St George's Golf Course and regains the modern coastline to follow the pebble beaches of Deal and Walmer opposite the treacherous Goodwin Sands. The Way passes Caesar's landing place, Walmer Castle (the official residence of the Lord Warden of the Cinque Ports) and climbs on to the high chalk cliffs of Kingsdown and St Margaret's Bay.

At Dover the NDW is followed to Folkestone where there are two alternative routes of the Saxon Shore Way. The Downs alternative passes close to Cheriton where the Eurotunnel Exhibition Centre is located. Apart from numerous models, videos and a section of a shuttle train, the exhibition has a working model of the whole Channel Tunnel terminal area. The main route follows the coast through Sandgate and Hythe, and after rejoining the Downs Alternative leaves the Royal Military Canal to reach Court-at-Street, Aldington and Bilsington Priory before entering the National Nature Reserve of Hamstreet Woods. After Hamstreet the Way follows the Royal Military Canal again for a while to Appledore with its bulb farm (Kent's answer to the Netherlands) before crossing the Isle of Oxney to reach the River Rother. This is followed for 3.5 miles (5.6 km), crossing the Kent/East Sussex border and entering the medieval hill town of Rye.

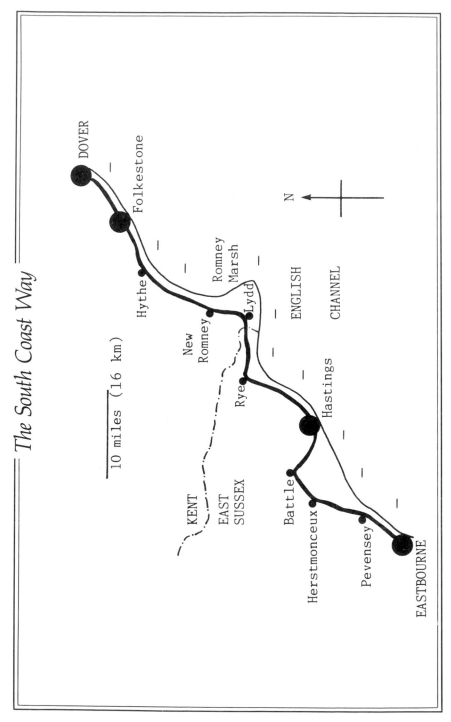

The South Coast Way

10 miles (16 km)

N

DOVER
Folkestone
Hythe
New Romney
Romney Marsh
Lydd
Rye
Hastings
Battle
Herstmonceux
Pevensey
EASTBOURNE

KENT
EAST SUSSEX
ENGLISH CHANNEL

The South Coast Way

Information

Length	81 miles (130 km)
Start & finish	Dover (Castle, Grid ref. TR 324419)
	Eastbourne (Pier, Grid ref. TV 618989)
Details of route	Dover – Folkestone – Hythe – Royal Military Canal – Dymchurch – New Romney – Lydd – Rye – Winchelsea – Hastings – Battle – Herstmonceux – Pevensey – Eastbourne
Counties traversed	Kent, East Sussex
Nature of route	A Recreational path devised by Laurence Main by linking rights of way and short road sections
Average duration	5 days
Landscape	Coastal towns, cliff tops, seashore, sea wall, Royal Military Canal, light railway, Romney Marsh, castles
AONB & Heritage Coast	Hastings Country Park is within the High Weald AONB. The route follows the 4 miles (6.4 km) of the Dover–Folkestone Heritage Coast
Date of opening	The Guidebook was published in 1980
Waymarking	There are no special South Coast Way signposts but the public rights of way used are waymarked with the standard yellow and blue arrows
Navigation	Grade B. Some fairly long sections on road and seashore are very easy to follow. Romney Marsh requires care in navigation
Maps	O.S. Landranger 1:50 000, Nos 179, 189, 199
	O.S. Pathfinder 1:25 000, Nos TR: 24/34, 13/23, 01/02; TQ: 81/91, 61/71, 60/70; TV 49/59/69
Linking LDPs	The South Coast Way links the NDW at Dover with the SDW and the Wealdway at Eastbourne
Shared LDPs	The Saxon Shore Way and the South Coast Way share the same route for the 12 miles (19.3 km) between Dover and Hythe
Other LDPs	The South Coast Way meets the Sussex Border Path at Rye where the latter path terminates
Transport	Public transport presents few problems on this LDP. There are main line British Rail stations at Dover, Folkestone, Rye, Winchelsea, Hastings, Battle, Pevensey and Eastbourne. The Romney, Hythe and Dymchurch Light Railway operates during the summer months between Hythe, Dymchurch and New Romney. There is a frequent bus service operating throughout

the year between Dover and Folkestone (service 90/90A) and between Folkestone, Hythe, Dymchurch, New Romney, Lydd, Rye, Winchelsea, Hastings, Bexhill, Pevensey Bay and Eastbourne (service 11/12)

Accommodation
There are youth hostels near to the route at Dover, Hastings (Guestling) and Eastbourne (Beachy Head). There are several camp sites including those at Folkestone, Hythe, New Romney, Rye, Hastings, Battle and Pevensey Bay. There is an abundance of accommodation of all types along the route

Guidebook
A South Coast Way. A Walker's Guide by Laurence Main (1980), Thornhill Press (24 Mooreland Road, Cheltenham, Glos). 45 pages. This guide booklet consists of a series of strip maps at 1:25 000 annotated with points of interest. There are details of accommodation, public transport and other facilities. The publication is illustrated with pen and ink drawings

Shorter walks based on the South Coast Way
The Romney Marsh Preservation Society and Shepway Council working with a Countryside Commission grant reclaimed many footpaths on Romney Marsh during the late 1980s. More than 30 miles (48 km) of footpaths are now passable and are waymarked with oak posts bearing a green disc portraying a marsh sheep (some of these will be seen whilst walking the South Coast Way across Romney Marsh). A folder containing details of 6 circular walks from 5 to 9.5 miles (8 to 15.3 km) is available free from the Tourist Information Centre, Harbour Street, Folkestone, Kent CT20 1QN (enclose an SAE)

Guided walks
See under Saxon Shore Way

Deviations
Work on the Channel Tunnel at Dover/Folkestone may necessitate minor changes to this route in the future. See under NDW – Deviations

Description

The South Coast Way is the brainchild of the walker and author Laurence Main. It is an unofficial route in every sense of the term, being conceived, walked and referenced by one individual. There is only one guidebook to the route. It is another fine example of the sort of long distance walking route that anyone can devise simply using map and compass and linking together existing rights of way.

The South Coast Way commences at Dover, the Gateway to England, with a visit to the castle. The route follows that of both the NDW and the Saxon Shore Way as it wanders through the streets of the world's busiest international passenger port and climbs on to Shakespeare Cliff. This is so named because the bard was thought to have had it in mind when writing the tragedy of *King Lear* ('The country near Dover. Horrible steep'). In the late 1980s this area along the chalk cliffs was transformed as the construction of the Channel Tunnel progressed. A special village has been built to accommodate the construction workers and the area is a hive of activity. A few public footpaths have been temporarily closed but the cliff-top path which carries the three LDPs has not been affected. Eventually the whole area is to be re-landscaped. The path approaches a rifle range (where there is a diversion if the red flag is flying) and the Way then descends to Folkestone. On a clear day the coast of France is visible. Walkers looking for a little variety may want to cross over to France to sample some of the long distance paths (or 'Grandes Randonnées') in that country. There is a very extensive network of G R trails in France, amounting to some 25 000 miles (40 250 km) in all; the nearest is just 21 miles (33.8 km) away on the coast of northern France.

The South Coast Way takes the Marine Walk out of Folkestone and then follows Sandgate Esplanade to reach the Royal Military Canal. This 25-mile (40.3 km) waterway was built in 1805 during the Napoleonic Wars when the country was threatened by invasion from the French. The most likely site for a landing was considered to be Romney Marsh and to protect this area the canal was built and guarded by guns and patrolled by boats. After the defeat of the French, no commercial use could be found for the canal, but it remains navigable to this day and is a splendid recreational asset for the area. The canal leads into Hythe, the start of the Romney, Hythe and Dymchurch Railway. This 15-inch-gauge light railway, opened in 1927–8, is the longest miniature railway ever built. The line runs for 13.5 miles (21.7 km) from Hythe to Dymchurch, New Romney and Dungeness. The RH & DR owns a superb fleet of one-third scale steam and diesel locomotives, and a round trip over the entire line takes nearly three hours. The railway is open from March to October (for further details contact RHDR – see Useful Addresses).

After Hythe the route soon leaves the Royal Military Canal and follows the shoreline for several miles, passing Dymchurch with its extensive sandy beach and St Mary's Bay. At New Romney the path diverts inland to Lydd which has a splendid thirteenth-century church, the Cathedral of Kent. Several Martello towers are passed along this coast. A chain of such forts was built between Folkestone and Seaford Head around 1810 by the Royal Engineers as defensive structures

The village signpost at Battle, East Sussex (South Coast Way). The settlement grew up around Battle Abbey, built on the site of the Battle of Hastings

against the feared French invasion. They are named after the Torre della Martella in Corsica, on which the design was based. The Way crosses Romney Marsh, an interesting and exciting traverse to the picturesque town of Rye. Romney Marsh, an area of 45 000 acres, is a maze of dykes and drainage ditches with a strange, remote atmosphere, once the notorious haunt of smugglers. It is the home of giant marsh frogs, introduced from Hungary in the 1930s. Rye is one of the Cinque Ports although it now lies two miles from the sea, the river having long since silted up. It was made well known by E.F. Benson, a one-time mayor of Rye, who wrote of it as Tilling in the Mapp and Lucia novels.

The route continues via the isolated ruins of Henry VIII's Camber Castle to the outskirts of Winchelsea, a thirteenth-century walled town situated on a hill, and then samples another 3-mile (4.8 km) section of the tranquil Royal Military Canal. The terrain changes abrubtly as the steep cliffs and deep 'glens' of Hastings Country Park are traversed for some 4 miles (6.4 km) to the popular seaside town of Hastings. The country park, 580 acres in extent, is one of the highlights of the walk. Much of it has been designated as a Site of Special Scientific Interest (SSSI) on account of its unique geology and flora. The yellow gorse which grows in profusion on the cliffs has been taken as the symbol of the park.

After Hastings the South Coast Way, despite its title, leaves the sea for over 20 miles (32.2 km) to Pevensey. The first destination after Hastings is Battle, the major historical attraction of the walk. The town grew up around Battle Abbey, founded by William the Conqueror on the site of the Battle of Hastings. From here the Way continues to Herstmonceaux Castle which for many years from 1957 was the home of the Royal Greenwich Observatory. The walls of Pevensey Castle are one of the finest examples of Roman building in the country, built around AD 250 to form one of the forts of the Saxon Shore. Within the walls is a smaller fortress, Norman in origin. The final section of the route is a 5-mile (8 km) walk along the sands to Eastbourne. The South Downs at the foot of Beachy Head are reached at the end of the 3-mile (4.8 km) long promenade.

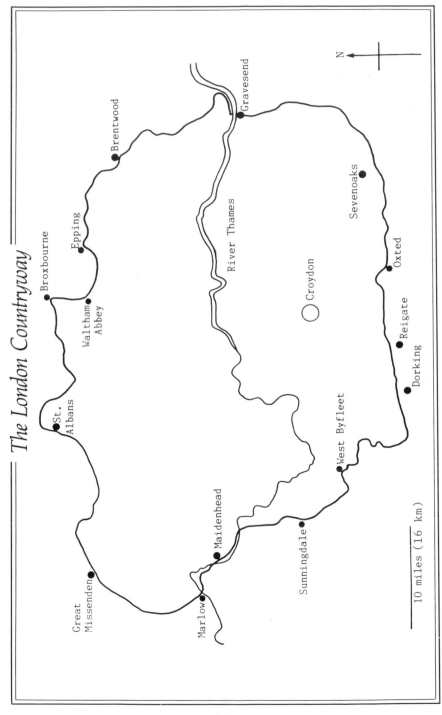

The London Countryway

Great Missenden

St. Albans

Broxbourne

Waltham Abbey

Epping

Brentwood

Gravesend

Sevenoaks

River Thames

Oxted

Croydon

Reigate

Dorking

West Byfleet

Maidenhead

Marlow

Sunningdale

N

10 miles (16 km)

The London Countryway

Information

Length	205 miles (330 km)
Start & finish	Box Hill (Stepping Stones, Grid ref. TQ 173513) A circular route
Details of route	Box Hill – Horsley – West Byfleet – Sunningdale – Windsor – Marlow – West Wycombe – Great Missenden – Ashley Green – Kings Langley – St Albans – Brookmans Park – Broxbourne – Theydon Bois – Bentley – West Horndon – East Tilbury – Sole Street – Borough Green – Ide Hill – Hurst Green – Merstham – Box Hill
Counties traversed	Surrey, Berkshire, Buckinghamshire, Hertfordshire, Essex and Kent
Nature of route	A Recreational path devised by Keith Chesterton and developed with assistance from members of the Long Distance Walkers Association. The route circumnavigates the capital by linking existing public rights of way
Average duration	14 days
Landscape	Downland, farmland, woodland, country parks, villages and towns, fenland, river and canal
AONBs	The route passes through three Areas of Outstanding Natural Beauty, viz. the Surrey Hills AONB, the Chilterns AONB and the Kent Downs AONB
Date of opening	The first guidebook to the London Countryway was published in 1976
Waymarking	Except in one or two places there are no specific London Countryway signs along the route. The public rights of way followed are usually waymarked with standard yellow (for footpaths) and blue (for bridleways) arrows
Navigation	Grade C
Maps	O.S. Landranger 1:50 000, Nos 165, 166, 167, 175, 177, 186, 187, 188
Shared LDPs	The London Countryway follows the route of the NDW for about 18 miles (29 km) between the A22 near Gravelly Hill and Hackhurst Downs, west of Dorking. The Thames Path and the London Countryway are co-incident for much of the way between Windsor and Marlow (13 miles; 20.9 km). The Countryway follows the line of the Epping

Forest Centenary Walk from Epping Forest Youth Hostel (High Beach) to Epping (about 4 miles; 6.4 km). The Wealdway and the London Countryway share the same route between Gravesend and Sole Street in Kent (5 miles; 8 km). Finally, the London Countryway follows the line of the Greensand Way for about 12 miles (19 km) between Ightham Mote and Limpsfield High Chart in Kent

Other LDPs   The London Countryway on its journey around London meets the start of the Essex Way at Epping and the start of the Saxon Shore Way at Gravesend. The Vanguard Way is crossed on Limpsfield High Chart at the Surrey/Kent border

Transport   There are over 30 British Rail stations on or near the route of the Countryway as well as a couple of London Underground stations. Train services to central London operate through all of these stations. There are also many bus services in the area. The London Countryway is therefore ideal for walking in daily stages, using public transport to reach the start of the day's section and returning to a home base at the end of the day. Alternatively, public transport can often be used to return to a car left at the start of a section

Accommodation   There are several youth hostels on or close to the London Countryway: Tanners Hatch in Surrey, Windsor, Bradenham in the Chilterns, St Albans, Epping Forest, Kemsing in Kent (some distance off route) and Crockham Hill, also in Kent, east of Hurst Green

Guidebook   *A Guide to the London Countryway* by Keith Chesterton (1978; second edition 1981), Constable. 280 pages. Hardback. The walk is divided into 22 stages, varying in length from 7 miles (11.3 km) to 13 miles (20.9 km), each section ending at a point where public transport is available. There is a detailed route description and a separate text describing places of interest and the terrain encountered. The route is marked on black and white 1:100 000 maps but the most intricate sections are provided with detailed sketch maps at 1:25 000. Adequate information on public transport and accommodation is included. The book is illustrated with a number of black and white photographs

Guided walks   See under Saxon Shore Way, North Downs Way and Essex Way

Deviations   The building of the M25 Orbital Motorway in the

early 1980s has necessitated the re-routing of small
sections of this LDP

Description

The London Countryway is a continuous LDP through the countryside
around London. The route completely encircles the capital and is the
only circular walk featured in this book. The Countryway was the idea
of Keith Chesterton, one-time chairman of the Long Distance Walkers
Association, who, having discovered that there was a circular walking
route around Paris (the GR 1 or Tour de l'Ile de France: 376 miles;
605 km), was determined to create a trail around the British capital.
Much of the work on developing the path was undertaken by numerous
members of the Long Distance Walkers Association who walked and
described several alternative paths. Five years elapsed between the original conception in 1971 and the production of the first privately published booklet describing the walk; an indication of the work involved in
such a project and the thoroughness with which the task was undertaken. The walk fired the imagination of many people and the popular-
ity of the route was proved by the appearance of a second edition of the
booklet in 1977, followed by the publication of a full-length hardback
Constable guide in 1978.

The route of the London Countryway covers the Kent and Surrey
hills, Surrey heathland, Thames valley, the Chilterns, Epping Forest and
Essex farmland, parkland and coastal plain. The furthest point on the
route from the centre of London is at West Wycombe, some 31 miles
(49.9 km) from Charing Cross. Waltham Abbey, only 13 miles (20.9 km)
from Charing Cross, is the closest the Countryway comes to the capital.
Despite its close proximity to the metropolis the London Countryway
is, with the exception of short stretches through Windsor, St Albans and
Gravesend, very much a rural path.

A circular walk of this nature can of course be started and finished at
any convenient point. However, the guidebook considers Box Hill in
Surrey an appropriate starting place. The walk is described in a clock-
wise direction. This is in fact the traditional way to tackle a circular walk;
some superstitious ramblers consider anti-clockwise to be the 'devil's
way'. From the stepping stones over the River Mole the London Countryway follows the NDW to Hackhurst Downs and then on through
Sheepleas, beech woodland rich in wild flowers, to reach East Horsley
railway station. The next stage is flatter and less wild, skirting a golf
course and crossing Ockham and Wisley Commons to pass the Royal
Horticultural Society's Gardens at Wisley and follow the Wey Navigation to West Byfleet. A second old canal (the Basingstoke Canal) is

*The Copper Horse Statue of George III, erected at the end of the 'Long Mile'
in Windsor Great Park in 1831*

Right *The Roman remains of Leptis Magna in Windsor Great Park.
Brought from Libya, they were re-erected here in 1827*

followed for 2 miles (3.2 km) before a crossing of two large commons: Horstell Common and the wilder and barer Chobham Common leading to Sunningdale. Chobham Common is 1600 acres of heathland, much of it a nature reserve well known for its wildlife.

The next section is through some of the finest parkland in Britain, the immense Windsor Great Park, passing the impressive artificial lake of Virginia Water, the Roman ruins of Leptis Magna, the 100 ft (30.5 m) totem pole (a gift from the Indians of Vancouver Island to celebrate the centenary of British Columbia) and the famous Copper Horse Statue of George III. The dead-straight Long Mile is followed to Windsor Castle. The town and castle of Windsor with their many places of interest merit a day's exploration.

The River Thames is followed from Windsor to Marlow, heralding the start of the Chilterns which are traversed for the next 30 miles (48.3 km) of the route. The Chilterns are a range of low but often steep-sided hills, an area of beechwoods and narrow valleys. The first destination is the picturesque Buckinghamshire village of West Wycombe with nearby Wycombe House (National Trust), the Hell Fire Caves and the Mausoleum and church on the hill overlooking the village. The 8 miles (12.9 km) to Great Missenden are perhaps the most strenuous of the entire journey, climbing a succession of steep hills through the heart of the Chilterns. The route passes to the north of Chesham to Ashley Green and then on to follow a broad ridge between the Chess and Bulborne valleys to cross the Grand Union Canal at Kings Langley. The National Rose Society Gardens are passed en route to St Albans, the Roman city of Verulamium. Here there is much of interest including the cathedral, thought to be the site of the execution of the

first Christian martyr in Britain in AD 209, a number of Roman ruins and the attractive, landscaped Verulamium Park through which the Countryway passes.

The route crosses Hertfordshire's unspectacular but pleasant countryside, passing several villages and country pubs, North Mymms Park (of Little Miss Muffet fame) and the Swallowhole where the Mimmshall brook disappears into a hole in the ground. Navigational skills are tested through Wormley Wood to reach Broxbourne and the Lea Valley Regional Park. This is followed to Waltham Abbey, the last to surrender to Henry VIII during the time of the dissolution of the monasteries. The church here is famous for its Pre-Raphaelite decorations. The Countryway continues to High Beach for a crossing of Epping Forest, a superb stretch of ancient, deciduous woodland close to London. Little-used country paths cross Essex from church to church between Theydon Bois and Bentley near Brentwood. Two country parks (Weald Park and Thorndon Park) lead to the flat Essex Fens, an eerie land of dykes and wide skyscapes. A crossing of the lonely Essex Marshes terminates in the industrial surroundings of Tilbury where a ferry over to Gravesend is necessary to continue the walk.

The Countryway has now entered Kent and for the first few miles follows the Wealdway to Sole Street. The next stage is over the chalk of the North Kent Downs, much less well known than the main ridge of the North Downs, but attractive country nevertheless. The orchards of Kent around Borough Green lead to the parkland of Fairlawne and the Tudor Ightham Mote, the most complete small manor house in Kent. This part timber-framed building owned by the National Trust is completely surrounded by a moat. The next 12 miles (19.3 km) to the county boundary with Surrey are shared by the Greensand Way. After Hurst Green to the south of Limpsfield the route heads north-west to the beautiful secluded Marden valley before reaching the NDW again just before the A22 near Gravelly Hill. This leads back to Box Hill Country Park (National Trust), the start of the walk.

The London Countryway passes through areas rich in historical, literary and artistic associations, some of the finest parkland in the country and some of its greatest buildings. Among the royalty and famous people associated with the places around London visited by the Countryway are Charles II, Victoria, Elizabeth I, Kings Harold and Edmond, Lord Nelson, Sir Walter Raleigh, Disraeli, Dickens, Octavia Hill (co-founder of the National Trust) and many more. The buildings of national importance passed en route include Windsor Castle, St George's Chapel, St Alban's Cathedral, Waltham Abbey, Chartwell (home of Sir Winston Churchill) and Cookham Church (houses Stanley Spencer's painting of the Last Supper). There is much to interest the walker on this very varied route around the nation's capital.

Virginia Water, the large artificial lake in Windsor Great Park, created by the Duke of Cumberland during the 18th century

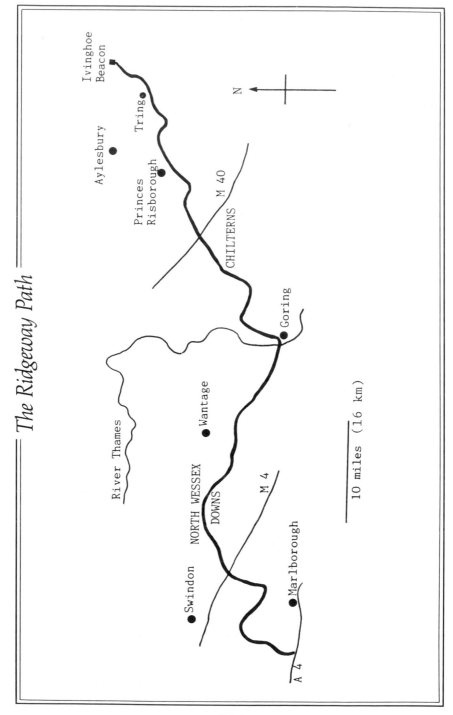

The Ridgeway Path

Ivinghoe Beacon

Aylesbury

Tring

Princes Risborough

M 40

CHILTERNS

Goring

River Thames

Wantage

NORTH WESSEX DOWNS

M 4

Swindon

Marlborough

A 4

N

10 miles (16 km)

The Ridgeway Path

Information

Length	85 miles (137 km)
Start & finish	Overton Hill, near Avebury (Grid ref. SU 118681) Ivinghoe Beacon (Grid ref. SP 960168)
Details of route	Overton Hill – Barbury Park – Liddington Castle – Wayland's Smithy – Uffington Castle – Streatley – Goring – Grim's Ditch – Icknield Way – Princes Risborough – Chequers – Wendover – Tring – Ivinghoe Beacon
Counties traversed	Wiltshire, Oxfordshire, Hertfordshire, Buckinghamshire, Berkshire and Bedfordshire
Nature of route	National Trail. Managed and funded by the Countryside Commission. The first 43 miles (69.2 km) from Overton Hill to Streatley are along a continuous bridleway and hence can be followed on horseback or by cycle as well as on foot
Average duration	One week
Landscape	Chalk downland and woodland. Prehistoric hill forts, burial chambers, ancient trackways and other antiquities abound. The final section is over the wooded Chiltern Hills
AONBs	The Trail is entirely within Areas of Outstanding Natural Beauty, viz. the North Wessex Downs AONB and the Chilterns AONB
Date of opening	29 September 1973 at an official ceremony on Coombe Hill
Waymarking	The Countryside Commission acorn symbol. There are numerous wooden Ridgeway signposts and some concrete plinths
Navigation	Grade A
Maps	O.S. Landranger 1:50 000, Nos 165, 173, 174, 175 O.S. Pathfinder 1:25 000, Nos SP: 81/91, 60/70, 80/90; SU: 69/79, 28/38, 48/58, 68/78, 07/17, 27/37
The Icknield Way	The eastern section of the Ridgeway Path follows for considerable stretches this prehistoric trackway which originally ran from Wells-next-the-Sea in Norfolk to join with the ancient Ridgeway track at Goring
Linking LDPs	The Ridgeway Path links the Icknield Way (a 100-mile; 161 km modern LDP following the line of the ancient trackway) at Ivinghoe Beacon to the Wessex

Ridgeway (a 100-mile; 161 km LDP from Overton Hill to Lyme Regis) and also to the Wessex Way (a 103-mile; 166 km route from Overton Hill to Swanage)

Other LDPs

The North Bucks Way (a 35-mile; 56 km LDP from Chequers Knap near Great Kimble) starts on the Ridgeway Path in the vicinity of Princes Risborough. The D'Arcy Dalton Way (64 miles; 103 km to Wormleighton reservoir on the Oxford Canal) starts at Wayland's Smithy on the Ridgeway Path. The Ridgeway is intersected by the Thames Path at Goring and by the Oxfordshire Way (65 miles; 105 km from Bourton-on-the-Water to Henley-on-Thames), King Alfred's Way (108 miles; 174 km from Portsmouth to Oxford) and the Wiltshire Way (a 162-mile; 261 km circular walk from Salisbury). Note: brief details of walks mentioned but not featured in this book can be found in the *Long Distance Walker's Handbook* by Barbara Blatchford & John Margetts (4th edition, 1990), published by A&C Black

Transport & accommodation

The Ridgeway Information and Accommodation Guide edited by D. Venner is available from Oxfordshire County Council (see Useful Addresses). As well as general information on the Ridgeway Path this publication also contains full details of bus and rail services and a list with addresses and telephone numbers of camp sites, youth hostels and B & B establishments along the way. Details of various 'village services' are also included. Recommended. It is updated annually.

The nearest British Rail station to Overton Hill is at Swindon, 13 miles (21 km) away, but there is a bus service from Swindon to Avebury which is only 2 miles (3.2 km) from the start of the Ridgeway Path. There is also a large car park at Avebury. Tring Railway Station is passed on the Ridgeway Path, 4 miles (6.4 km) before Ivinghoe Beacon at the end of the Trail. There are youth hostels at Court Hill (near Wantage), Streatley, Bradenham (3 miles; 4.8 km off route) and Ivinghoe

Guidebooks

1   *The Ridgeway* by Neil Curtis (1989). A joint publication between Aurum Press, the Countryside Commission and the Ordnance Survey. 144 pages. This is the new National Trail Guide and is a considerable improvement on the old official guide to the Ridgeway (HMSO, 1977, by Sean Jennett) which it replaces. The main advantage of buying this

book is that it contains the appropriate sections of the O.S. 1:25 000 maps with the route delineated in yellow. There is a route description as well as mileage charts, historical background, practical advice and some general accommodation and transport information. The day walker is also accommodated by the inclusion of 6 circular routes which contain sections of the Ridgeway Path. The text is illustrated with colour photographs. Recommended.

2   *The Ridgeway Path* by H.D. Westacott and mapped by Mark Richards (1982), Penguin. 107 pages. Detailed sketch maps of the route. There are sections on geology and wildlife, historical background, accommodation, transport and general advice. Places along the way and other points of interest are highlighted.

3   *The Oldest Road; An Exploration of the Ridgeway* by Fay Godwin and J.R.L. Anderson. (First published in 1975 by Wildwood House. Published by Whittet in 1987.) 200 pages. Archaeological sites and other places of interest are discussed in some detail. There is a good selection of accurate sketch maps and a section on the logistics of the walk, including the best ways to make use of a car to walk sections of the route. Grid references are given throughout the text. The photographs are of the usual high standard now expected of the well-known professional photographer and past President of the Ramblers' Association, Fay Godwin.

Shorter walks based on the Ridgeway   Leaflets describing short circular walks based on the Ridgeway Path can be obtained from the Ridgeway Officer (see Useful Addresses under Oxfordshire County Council). These include walks based on Barbury Castle, Burderop Down, Smeathe's Ridge, the Ogbournes, Scutchamer Knob, West Ginge Down, Ashdown House, Wayland's Smithy, Ellesborough, Kimble and Ilsley

Guided walks   Oxfordshire County Council organise an extensive series of guided theme walks between April and October and many of these use sections of the Ridgeway Path. In addition a series of 10 Sunday walks is organised along the entire length of the Ridgeway Path. In this scheme there is usually a walk every other Sunday between May and October (except August). A coach is provided on each occasion to take the walker from his/her car, which is parked at the finishing point, out to the

Challenge walk

Vehicular use of the Ridgeway

start of the walk. The participants then walk back to their cars, a distance of 6–11 miles (9.7–17.7 km) An annual challenge walk is held along the western half of the Ridgeway from Marlborough to Streatley Youth Hostel. The event is usually held on the first weekend in May and the time limit for the 40 miles (64.4 km) is around 13 hours. Transport from Streatley to the start is normally provided. For details send an SAE to Ridgeway Enquiries, 7 Mowbray Drive, Tilehurst, Reading RH3 4XY or enquire from the Long Distance Walkers Association (see Useful Addresses)

The 40-mile (64.4 km) stretch between Overton Hill and Streatley is a legally designated byway over which 4-wheeled vehicles and motorcycles have right of access. At present a Code of Voluntary Restraint is in operation. All motorcyclists and motorists (other than those requiring access, disabled and emergency vehicles) have been asked to keep off the Ridgeway on Sundays and Bank Holidays between 1 May and 31 October, and after prolonged wet weather at any time of the year. However, in the autumn of 1989 the Countryside Commission requested the Secretary of State for the Environment to implement a traffic regulation order banning vehicular use on Sundays and Bank Holidays throughout the year, the 60 days most popular with pedestrians. This action followed a survey of the users of the National Trail and was thought by the Commission to be the only effective way of controlling the problems of the Ridgeway

Description

If the Thames Path and London Countryway can be considered to be walks through history, then the Ridgeway must surely be a walk through prehistory. The path follows part of an important prehistoric trading route which stretched from Norfolk across the chalk ridges of southern England to South Devon. From East Anglia to the Thames valley at Goring it was known as the Icknield Way and from thereon it became the Great Ridgeway, often considered to be the oldest road, being in use around 4000 years ago. Prehistoric relics abound, particularly on the first half of the Trail to the west of the Thames at Goring. A variety of earthworks, hill forts, burial mounds, menhirs and dolmens will be passed en route and the keen amateur archaeologist will find much to occupy him or herself on this downland walk. For much of the way the route follows a line of hills that are higher than the surrounding land and so the views are often far reaching across lowland plains and valleys.

The Ridgeway Path starts at the foot of Overton Hill on the A4, for many years the site of the Ridgeway Café. In the late 1980s there was considerable controversy over plans for the commercial exploitation of the area. Most walkers will first want to explore nearby Avebury, the site of Europe's largest stone circle, 450 yds (411 m) in diameter, enclosing an area of 30 acres. There are 98 sarsen stones in the circle, each weighing 40 tons. The circle was probably the work of the Windmill Hill people, a Neolithic tribe, in about 2600 BC. The stones were transported two miles over the Downs from Grey Wethers, an area near the Ridgeway Path where numerous sarsen stones are found. From Avebury a path leads to Silbury Hill, a huge artificial mound dating from the same period, and from here a permissive path can be taken to West Kenett Long Barrow. The whole area was an important centre of prehistoric life.

The Ridgeway Path climbs to the top of the Wiltshire Downs, now a National Nature Reserve and only descends twice (to the Og valley and for a crossing of the M4 motorway) in the 43 miles (69 km) to the Thames valley. This is high rolling downland, rich in history and crossed by a multitude of ancient tracks used by drovers in the eighteenth century to drive their stock to market. There are four iron age hill forts between Overton Hill and the Thames: Barbury Castle, site of a Saxon battle against the Britons in AD 556, Liddington Castle beloved of Richard Jeffries, Uffington Castle and Letcombe Castle (Segsbury Camp). Uffington is most famous for its white horse, a huge chalk figure probably dating from the iron age. Legend has it that nearby Dragon Hill is the site of the slaying of the dragon, the bare patch on the summit a result of the spilled beast's blood.

Numerous barrows are to be found along the way, the most well-known being that of Wayland's Smithy west of Uffington. The name is derived from a Saxon legend that Wayland, the blacksmith of the gods, would shoe a traveller's horse overnight if suitable payment was left at the barrow. Wayland's Smithy is a large, two-chambered neolithic long barrow dating from around 3000 BC. Twenty-two skeletons were discovered there on excavation.

The Romans also occupied this downland. Lowbury Hill is the site of a Roman temple and on nearby Roden Downs is a site of a burial ground dating from Roman times. In later years King Alfred left his mark on these hills with his defeat of the Danes at the Battle of Ashdown in AD 871. The nearby Blowingstone is where, it is said, he summoned his troops into battle. There are many ditches, banks, ancient field systems,

The Iron Age Hill Fort of Uffington on the Ridgeway. This scene was taken from near Wayland's Smithy. (Photograph courtesy of The Ramblers' Association)

strip lynchets and remains of old deserted villages which all tell a story of settlement and rural industry. The North Wessex Downs can be seen as a palimpsest on which the more recent writings have by no means obliterated the past.

Once across the Thames valley the Ridgeway Path follows for 3 miles (4.8 km) the raised earthbanks of Grim's Ditch, an iron age territorial boundary. The route also takes the ancient Icknield Way for many miles, passing the mysterious 'white mark' on Watlington Hill and on to pass underneath the M40 motorway near Beacon Hill Nature Reserve. The Icknield Way is incorporated into the modern road system near Princes Risborough, but just prior to this the Ridgeway Path leaves it to climb above Risborough Cop and proceeds through attractive woodland towards the Chequers estate, the official country retreat of the Prime Minister. Beechwoods are traversed over Coombe Hill to Wendover and the Ridgeway then continues to Tring, on the main line to Euston. There remains 4 more miles (6.4 km) over a series of chalk hills reminiscent of the open downland encountered on the first stages of the walk back in Wiltshire. After the steepest hill on the whole journey the Ridgeway Path finishes on the summit of Ivinghoe Beacon, the site of yet another iron age hill fort and a fine viewpoint.

The Ridgeway Path links the modern Icknield Way at Ivinghoe Beacon to the Wessex Ridgeway at Overton Hill. The Ridgeway Path therefore forms an 85-mile (137 km) section of an ultra-long-distance walking route from Great Yarmouth on the Norfolk coast to the Dorset coast at Lyme Regis, where it joins the South West Way to Minehead in North Devon. It is therefore possible to follow a continuous path on foot across the whole of southern England. The route, which is about 920 miles (1481 km) long, comprises the Weavers' Way (Great Yarmouth to Cromer), the Norfolk Coast Path and Peddars Way (Cromer to Knettishall Heath near Thetford), Icknield Way (Knettishall Heath to Ivinghoe Beacon), Ridgeway Path, Wessex Ridgeway (Overton Hill to Lyme Regis), and the South West Way following the coast via Land's End to Minehead. To the author's knowledge this mammoth journey has not yet been undertaken in one continuous walk. It would be a challenge and the walk of a lifetime for some adventurous soul.

The Thames Path

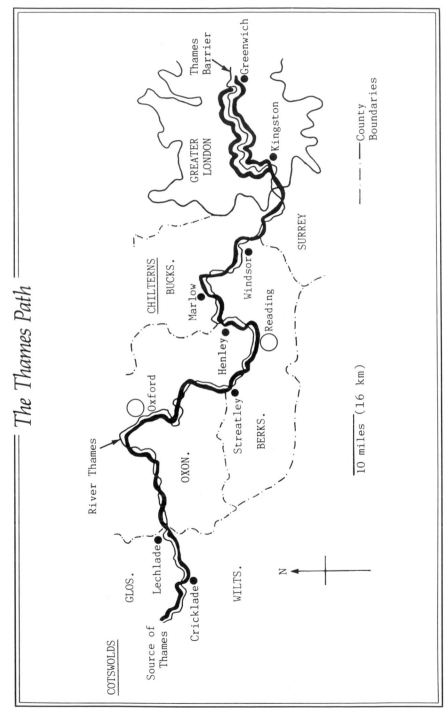

The Thames Path

Information

Length	180 miles (290 km)
Start & finish	Thames Barrier at Woolwich Reach, Greenwich (Grid ref. TQ 417794) Source of the River Thames near Kemble, Gloucestershire (Grid ref. ST 980994)
Details of route	Thames Barrier – Kew Bridge – Kingston – Hampton Court – Chertsey – Windsor – Maidenhead – Cookham – Marlow – Henley on Thames – Reading – Goring – Wallingford – Abingdon – Oxford – Bablock Hythe – Newbridge – Tadpole – Lechlade – Cricklade – the Source
Counties traversed	Greater London, Surrey, Berkshire, Buckinghamshire, Oxfordshire, Wiltshire, Gloucestershire
Nature of route	The 14th National Trail and the first one to follow the course of a river. It is to be developed, funded and managed by the Countryside Commission
Average duration	12–15 days
Landscape	Riverside towpath, cities and towns. The path passes through both urban and rural landscapes. A region rich in cultural and historical associations
AONBs	The Thames Path passes through the Chilterns AONB and terminates in the Cotswolds AONB
Date of opening	In 1981 the Countryside Commission funded a feasibility study on the possible designation of a trail along the Thames as a national LDP. In 1984 the Commission decided to go ahead with a path and appointed a project officer in June 1985 to work out the exact route. The final details of the proposed route were published by the Countryside Commission in April 1989. The approval of the Environment Secretary was obtained in the autumn of 1989. The Trail is expected to be officially opened in 1992, but a large percentage of the route can already be walked
Waymarking	The Thames Path, as a National Trail, will be waymarked using the Countryside Commission's acorn symbol
Navigation	Grade A. Very easy to follow
Maps	O.S. Landranger 1:50 000, Nos 177, 176, 175, 164, 163

O.S. Pathfinder 1:25 000, Nos TQ 47/57, 48/58, 27/37, 07/17, 06/16; SU: 87/97, 88/98, 68/78, 67/77, 48/58, 49/59, 29/39, 09/19; SP: 40/50, 20/30; ST: 89/99

Alternative route The Countryside Commission is seeking a dual bank route through London. From there on the path will follow either one bank of the river or the other

The Thames Walk It is possible to walk much of the route before the official opening of the Thames Path. The Ramblers' Association have published a guide to the Thames Walk, a 156-mile (251 km) route from Putney to the source (see Guidebooks). The problem is that the old towpath changes sides of the river many times and in the Thames Walk several deviations have been made to cope with missing ferries and footbridges. Furthermore a few diversions have been necessary in the Thames Walk to avoid a number of private estates. The route of the Thames Walk can be followed until the necessary bridges are built, rights of way created across certain private estates and the Thames Path officially opened. By May 1989 one major footbridge costing £350 000 had been erected over the Thames at Temple, near Marlow, saving a 1.5-mile (2.4 km) road detour

Shared LDPs The Thames Path and the London Countryway are co-incident between Windsor and Marlow, a distance of about 13 miles (20.9 km). *The Thames Valley Heritage Walk* (guidebook by Miles Jebb, Constable) follows the general line of the Thames Path for parts of the way between London and Oxford

Other LDPs The Ridgeway Path and the D'Arcy Dalton Way cross the Thames Path at Goring and Radcot Bridge respectively. The Oxfordshire Way ends its 65 miles (105 km) from Bourton-on-the-Water at Henley on Thames

Transport The Thames valley is well served by public transport of all kinds. British Rail or London buses can be used to reach the start of the route at the Thames Barrier. Kemble railway station is only about a mile from the source of the Thames in Gloucestershire. In between there are many other railway stations and bus services, making this an ideal path to complete in a number of separate day walks

Accommodation The two London youth hostels nearest to the Thames are in Carter Lane near St Paul's and at Earl's Court. Along the Trail there are youth hostels at Windsor, Streatley, Oxford and Inglesham (2 miles;

3.2 km from Lechlade on the Thames). The cities, towns and villages en route provide plenty of accommodation of all types and price ranges

Guidebooks

1 *A Guide to the Thames Path* by Miles Jebb (1988), Constable. 336 pages. PVC cover. The walk is described from Kew Bridge to the source of the Thames, a distance of 152 miles (245 km) in the upstream direction, and is divided into 15 stages ranging from 8.3 to 12.3 miles (13.4 to 19.8 km) in length. The text is accompanied by a number of black and white photographs as well as black and white Bartholomew maps at 1:100 000 with the route overlaid. Data is also provided on the downstream journey and there is plenty of information on accommodation, transport, approach by car and admission to buildings and gardens open to the public. The text is scholarly with a wealth of historical facts in addition to anthology sections containing a total of 65 prose extracts of numerous writers from Julius Caesar to Kenneth Grahame. The book also contains details of six circular walks based on the Thames Path. These vary in length from 6.1 to 12.8 miles (9.8 to 20.6 km).

2 *The Thames Walk* by David Sharp (first published 1985; revised edition 1990). Published by the Ramblers' Association. 64 pages. This describes a provisional 156-mile (251 km) walking route from Putney to the source. There are good-quality sketch maps showing the route and the deviations from the towpath required until the necessary bridges are erected and rights of way opened. There is a route description and places of interest are highlighted. Public transport possibilities are described and the background to the path is discussed. Note that in the revised 1990 edition of the guidebook to the Thames Walk, the route is described from the Thames Barrier to the Source.

3 *A Guide to London's Riverside* by Suzanne Ebel and Doreen Impey. Constable. This book provides a comprehensive description of the tidal Thames. A new edition will include details of the lower Thames Path and so will complement Miles Jebb's guidebook (see No. 1 above).

Deviation

The extraction sites for the proposed Jubilee Line Underground extension in London may threaten several Thames riverside paths. Whatever the outcome there will always be a path on at least one side of the river all the way through the capital

Description

The Thames is an unusual river in that one can walk along its banks for the whole of its length, from the tidal reaches in London to its source in the Gloucestershire Cotswolds. This is possible because there exists a towpath along nearly all of the 200 or so miles (320 km) from source to sea. Unfortunately this towpath frequently changes from bank to bank. It is this simple fact which has delayed the development of the towpath into a long distance route. There is a historical reason for the towpath continually changing sides. The Thames lacked a single effective authority until the late eighteenth century when the Conservators of the River Thames were given the responsibility for administering the river and creating a continuous towpath to facilitate the towing of barges. By that late date the land alongside the river was owned by various individuals and organisations, many of whom obstructed the laying of a towpath on their land. The problem was overcome by changing banks where necessary and using a series of bridges and ferries to cross the river. In the heyday of river navigation in the early nineteenth century, before the coming of the railways, the system worked well but with the decline of the Thames as a commercial highway, the ferries one by one ceased to operate.

The recreational potential of the Thames towpath has long been recognised. In the early 1950s the newly created National Parks Commission (now the Countryside Commission) included a walk along the Thames in a shortlist of proposed long distance walking routes for consideration. However, the cost of building the necessary bridges across the river was thought to be too high. There followed three decades of lobbying by the Ramblers' Association and the River Thames Society to persuade the powers that be to reconsider the Thames Path as a national long distance trail. Following a conference held at Windsor in 1973 by the River Thames Society, the Ramblers' Association decided to carry out their own survey of the route. After three years of effort by local RA groups the result of their labours, *The Thames Walk*, was published in 1977. In 1980 the Thames Water Authority gave its general support to the concept of a continuous footpath along the Thames. Faced with the support for a Thames Path from many quarters and with strong public opinion in favour of a path, the Countryside Commission decided to act during the mid-1980s and the result has been the development of a new National Trail. It has taken nearly 50 years to establish this new long distance route.

The Thames Path will commence at the Thames Barrier, near Greenwich. The Barrier, completed in the early 1980s, is London's main defence against the mighty power of the tidal river which has threatened to flood the capital on several occasions. It is the world's largest flood barrier, built at a cost of nearly £500 million. It spans a third of a mile across the river, its 10 separate gates pivoted and supported between 9 concrete piers which house the hydraulic machinery powering the gates. An impressive place to start a long distance walk.

The Thames Path will journey through the capital to Putney Bridge of Boat Race fame, on past the Royal Botanic Gardens at Kew and the great open space of Richmond Park, to reach Kingston. This is a very pleasant route out of the capital, a veritable *rus in urbe*. The next stop is Hampton Court with its famous palace and the river continues to the Thames Lock at Weybridge, where the Wey navigation is met. This 'canalised' river forms part of the Wey-South Path from Guildford to the South Downs, and a link to this LDP is possible by following the towpath south from Weybridge. Back on the Thames the Path continues to Chertsey and on to Staines and the meadows of Runnymede where the Magna Carta was signed by King John in 1215. More history at Windsor, and at the rear of Eton the river crosses the meadows of Brocas with fine views back to Windsor Castle.

The river approaches Maidenhead to pass under the rail bridge designed by Brunel to carry the Great Western Railway. Beyond is Boulters Lock and then Cookham with its twelfth-century church in which hangs Stanley Spencer's famous painting of the Last Supper. There is a small art museum in the village devoted to the works of Spencer. The Path crosses Cock Marsh (National Trust) and Winter Hill to enter Marlow. The chain bridge here, built in 1832, is a prototype of the famous Chain Bridge across the Danube in Budapest. The Thames valley is now at the foot of the sylvan Chilterns. The picturesque village of Hurley leads along a superb reach of the Thames to the white weatherboarded Hambledon Mill and on to Henley, famous for its Regatta. Sonning with its eighteenth-century bridge of 11 brick arches is passed en route for Reading. For such a large urban area the river bank remains largely rural and after Caversham Bridge the country is soon regained. And so to Purley, Whitchurch and Pangbourne to reach Goring. The river has cut a wide valley through the chalk downs at this point where the twin villages of Goring and Streatley are situated on either side of the river. They tend to be dormitory towns of Reading, Oxford and London and are sometimes irreverently referred to as 'Boring and Discretely'.

The Thames Path follows the Ridgeway Path for a while through the attractive villages of North and South Stoke, but when the Ridgeway turns off towards the Chilterns the Thames continues north to Wallingford and on through delightful country to Abingdon, with the spire of St Helen's church providing a prominent landmark. The towpath leads to Oxford with views over Christchurch Meadows and the spires and domes of the various Colleges. Up until Oxford the Thames is a well-used waterway much frequented by motor craft. Upstream from Oxford the river enters less well-known stretches where there is considerable peace and tranquillity. From here on there are no large towns to negotiate. Indeed for the next 20 miles (32 km) to Lechlade there are no villages or towns along the river. Bablock Hythe is the site of a once important Thames crossing. The Romans had a ford here and a ferry operated for many hundreds of years until the second half of this century. The river continues to St John's Lock, the highest on the Thames where the reclining statue of Father Thames is to be found.

The Thames towpath finally ends a mile above Lechlade. From here it is 10 miles (16 km) to the Roman village of Cricklade and then the infant Thames is followed for a further 12.5 miles (20 km) to its source north of the village of Kemble. Journey's end is marked with a simple inscribed stone erected by the Conservators of the Thames.

The Thames Path with its gentle gradients, well-surfaced paths and ease of access will almost certainly become one of the more well-used National Trails. The Thames valley has witnessed many of the great scenes in British history and the Path passes close to fine palaces, castles, churches, gardens and National Trust properties. The Countryside Commission plan to provide access for the disabled along several stretches of the Path and the walk will be suitable for families, youngsters and elderly people who may be daunted by many of the more strenuous long distance routes.

The Essex Way

Information

Length	81 miles (130 km)
Start & finish	Epping (Railway Station, Grid ref. TL 465012) Harwich (Quay, Grid ref. TM 259329) Note: The original Essex Way was 62 miles (100 km) long and ran from Epping to Dedham, Grid ref. TM 060333
Details of route	Epping – Toot Hill – Greensted Church – Chipping Ongar – Cannons Green – Willingale – Pepper's Green – Good Easter – Pleshey – Great Waltham – Chatham Green – Little Leighs – Fuller Street – Terling – Fairstead – White Notley – Cressing – Perry Green – Coggeshall – Great Tey – Ford Street – West Bergholt – Horkesley Heath – Boxted – Langham Hall – Dedham – Manningtree – Mistley – Bradfield – Wrabness – Ramsey – Little Oakley – Harwich
Counties traversed	Essex
Nature of route	A Recreational or Regional LDP devised and developed by the Essex Branch of the Council for the Protection of Rural England (CPRE) with assistance from members of the Ramblers' Association and from parish councils and Essex County Council. It is now managed by Essex County Council
Average duration	5–6 days
Landscape	Villages and towns, churches, green lanes, farmland, saltings, estuary, marsh, mudflats and coast
AONB	The Way passes through the Essex section of Dedham Vale AONB
Date of opening	The Essex Way was developed as a contribution to Euro Conservation Year 1971
Waymarking	Essex Way and CPRE signposts are found along the Way (usually white lettering on black plaques)
Navigation	Grade B/C
Maps	O.S. Landranger 1:50 000, Nos 167, 168, 169 O.S. Pathfinder 1:25 000, Nos TQ: 49/59; TL: 40/50, 60/70, 61/71, 81/91, 82; TL 92 & TM 02; TM: 03/13, 12/22
Extension	The Epping Forest Centenary Walk is 15 miles (24.2 km) in length running from Manor Park (Grid ref. TQ 419857) on the outskirts of London to

Epping Station, the start of the Essex Way. It is therefore possible to walk the entire length of Essex from London to the sea, a distance of 96 miles (155 km). Details of the Epping Forest Centenary Walk are available from the Chief Conservator of The Forest, The Warren, Loughton, Essex

Shared LDPs
For 2 miles (3.2 km) through West Bergholt the Essex Way follows the line of the Camuplodunum, a 25-mile (40 km) circular walk around Colchester (details from D. Kebble, 9 Shelley Road, Colchester CO3 4JN)

The Epping Forest Centenary Walk follows the London Countryway through Epping Forest for about 4 miles (6.4 km)

Other LDPs
The Essex Way crosses three other LDPs in Essex:
1   St Peter's Way, a 45-mile (72.5 km) walk from Chipping Ongar (Essex Way) to Bradwell-on-Sea.
2   Three Forests Way, a 60-mile (97 km) circular walk linking Epping, Hatfield and Hainhault forests.
3   Essex Clayway, 28 miles (45 km) linking the Essex Way at Coggeshall to St Peter's Way at Mundon.

Details of these three LDPs from Fred Matthews, Glen View, London Road, Abridge, Essex.

The Painters Way (24 miles; 39 km, from Sudbury in Suffolk through Constable and Gainsborough country) finishes at Manningtree Station where there is a short link route to the Essex Way. Details of the Painters Way from Hugh R.P. Turner, Peddar Publications, Croft End Cottage, Bures, Suffolk.

Transport
The start of the Essex Way is at Epping Station (London Underground – Central Line) and the walk finishes in Harwich where there is a British Rail station with services to London. In between there is a Central Line station at Chipping Ongar (mile 7 from Epping) and British Rail stations at White Notley (mile 34), Manningtree (mile 66) and Mistley (mile 68). There are several bus routes along the way (details in the guidebook)

Accommodation
There are youth hostels in Epping Forest (High Beach) and Harlow for the start of the Way and also at Colchester to the south of Dedham. Enquiries for B & B and hotel accommodation may be made to Colchester Information Centre, 4 Trinity Street, Tel. 0206 46379

Guidebook
The Essex Way, A Long Distance Walk from Epping to Harwich by Fred Matthews and Harry Bitten (3rd edition, fully revised 1984). 24 pages. A joint

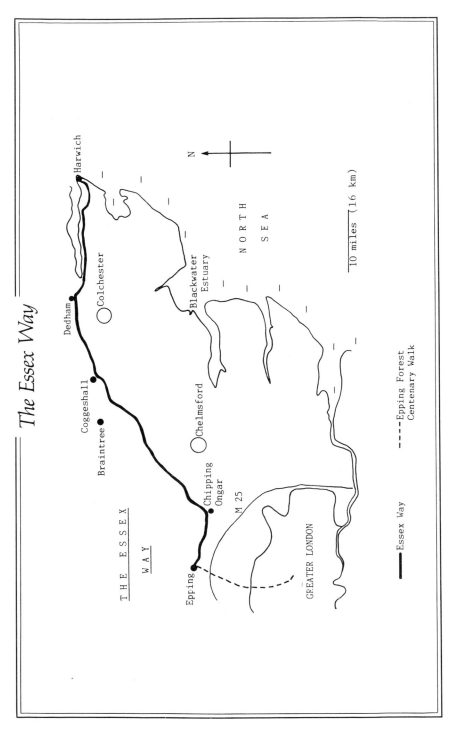

The Essex Way

Harwich

N

NORTH SEA

10 miles (16 km)

Dedham

Colchester

Blackwater Estuary

Coggeshall

Braintree

Chelmsford

Epping Forest Centenary Walk

THE ESSEX
WAY

Chipping Ongar

M 25

Epping

GREATER LONDON

----- Epping Forest Centenary Walk

——— Essex Way

publication of CPRE and Matthews/Bitten Publications. The booklet consists of a very detailed and reliable description of the route divided into 7 stages. There are sketch maps (at about 1:70 000) and a number of pen and ink drawings. Places of interest are mentioned and there is detailed transport information. The guide can be obtained from Fred Matthews, Glen View, London Road, Abridge, Essex

Shorter walks based on the Essex Way

Fred Matthews also publishes guidebooks to shorter walks in West Essex and in Epping Forest. Details from the above address

Guided walks

The local Rambler groups in Essex are very active and may include the Essex Way and other LDPs in the county in their programme of walks. Contact the Ramblers' Association for details

Description

Essex is fortunate in having an extensive interlocking network of long distance footpaths, many of which are detailed above. Much of the credit for the establishment of this network must go to Fred Matthews and his colleagues of the Ramblers' Association groups in Essex. They have devised, walked and published a number of routes in the county and have expended much effort to ensure that the footpaths are walkable and unobstructed. The oldest and best established of these is the Essex Way, from the outskirts of London right across the county to the sea at the port of Harwich.

Essex is very different in character to Kent and the other counties to the south of the Thames. It lacks the great chalk ridges of the North and South Downs and the impressive sea cliffs of Seaford and Dover, but the bird-filled creeks and marshlands of its coastline and the wide skyscapes and golden cornfields of its interior have a subtle, tranquil beauty. The Essex Way stretches from the medieval Epping Forest in the south-west of the county to Dedham Vale and the Stour Estuary, Constable country in the north-east. On its journey it links many of the picturesque villages and noble churches that are such a characteristic of this rural county. So much of the subtle charm of Essex is missed by the motorist with his eye to the road; the true nature of the county is only revealed to the patient and observant foot traveller.

The Essex Way starts its journey to the coast from Epping on the outskirts of the forest. Epping Forest covers an area of around 6000 acres and is a remnant of the Great Forest of Waltham which at one time covered much of the southern part of Essex. The Forest was preserved for the enjoyment of the general public by the efforts of one Thomas

This most attractive Cistercian Abbey at Coggeshall is passed on the route of the Essex Way

The half-timbered Paycocke's House in Coggeshall was built in c.1500 by a wealthy cloth merchant, John Paycocke (Essex Way)

Willingale, a Loughton man who in the nineteenth century faced impri-
sonment in his attempts to save the Forest from enclosures and development. Eventually he was supported by the Commons Preservation
Society and the City of London and the result of their combined efforts
was the passing of the Epping Forest Act by Parliament in 1878. To
celebrate the 100th anniversary of the Act's passing, Fred Matthews and
the West Essex Group of the Ramblers' Association devised the Epping
Forest Centenary Walk, a route of some 15 miles (24.2 km) through the
full length of the Forest. This walk stretches from the outskirts of
London at Manor Park near Forest Gate (one of the original 'gates' of
the Forest) to Epping for the start of the Essex Way. It is strongly
recommended that you include this traverse of Epping Forest in the full
walk across Essex.

From Epping the Essex Way proceeds through the woods of Garnon
Bushes to Greensted Church near Chipping Ongar. The church is of
great historical significance, being the only wooden church in the country remaining from Saxon times and probably the oldest wooden church
in the world. The earliest church on the site was built in the seventh
century and was enlarged in AD 845 to form the wooden Saxon church
still here today. It is a shrine to St Edmund, the Saxon king murdered by
the Danes in AD 870 and later buried at Bury St Edmunds. Chipping
Ongar, an ancient market town, also has a fine church as well as the
remains of a castle. Jane Taylor, the writer of children's poems including
'Twinkle, twinkle little star', lived in Ongar in the nineteenth century.

The Way continues via the Roding valley to Willingale, notable for
its two churches in one churchyard. Perhaps rather surprisingly both
churches are still in use today. Legend has it that the reason for the two
churches is that two sisters quarrelled and each built her own church.
This is, however, unlikely to be the case as the two churches were built
in different periods about 200 years apart. The real reason why the two
churches were originally built will probably remain a matter for specu-
lation. From Willingale a delightful green lane, that of Pepper's Green,
leads to the village of Good Easter. The green lane is one of several on
the route, Essex being fortunate in possessing around 400 miles
(644 km) of these secluded, peaceful byways. Good Easter is also the
start of the aptly named Two Seasons Way, a 30-mile (48.3 km) walk to
the village of Cold Christmas. This route was surveyed in 1985 to mark
the Golden Jubilee of the Ramblers' Association (details from Fred Matthews, see address above).

The River Chelmer is reached at Great Waltham, a pleasant village
possessing a fine fourteenth-century inn. It was a centre for vine grow-
ing in Roman times. Through Langley's Park and on via Chatham
Green, Little Leighs and Fuller Street to Terling, the home of Edward
Strutt in the nineteenth century, the pioneer of modern milk production

Pargeting on the walls of old buildings is a common site in Essex villages; this fine example is to be found in Coggeshall

Dedham High Street. The town, which is reached on the Essex Way, has many associations with the Constable family and the paintings of John Constable

Langham Church, Essex. One of Constable's famous paintings, 'Glebe Farm', was painted from a spot just to the north of this church

who built up one of the finest herds of Fresians in the country. Terling is a most attractive village having a fine example of a smock mill. And so to Coggeshall, a conservation area where there are several ornate houses. A slight detour into the town is required to visit Paycocke's House, a half-timbered house built in 1500 by John Paycocke, a wealthy cloth merchant (National Trust). The route passes Coggeshall's beautiful Cistercian abbey and nearby watermill.

The Way passes through Great Tey and follows the River Colne for a short while on its way to West Bergholt, Horkesley Heath and Boxted with its Norman church. Langham Hall is passed on the way to Dedham. This is John Constable country and Langham was the setting for *The Glebe Farm* painted in 1826/7 (National Gallery). Langham presents one of the finest views down into Dedham valley and it was from here that Constable painted the famous *Dedham Vale*. Dedham village has an old-world atmosphere and contains many notable Tudor and Georgian houses. The village and its surrounding fields appear in several of Constable's paintings including *Dedham Lock and Mill* painted in 1820 and the equally famous *Cornfield* (National Gallery). The artist was born in nearby East Bergholt and attended the grammar school in Dedham, now two private houses. Many of the places associated with Constable can be visited on foot from Dedham, including the most famous site of all, Flatford Mill, of *Haywain* fame. Sir Alfred Mannings, one time President of the Royal Academy, also lived near Dedham. His home, Castle House, is open to the public and contains a collection of his paintings and drawings.

The original Essex Way finished at Dedham but today it extends eastwards for a further 19 miles (30.6 km) mainly along the River Stour estuary. It is this river that divides Essex from its northern neighbour, Suffolk. The river, once noted for its numerous watermills, is today an important source of water for South Essex. After the industrial areas around Manningtree and Mistley the route resumes its former tranquillity over marshland, sea wall and Stour and Copperas Wood Reserves. It is a good place from which to observe wildfowl in the estuary and a hide has been provided for this purpose. The Essex Way terminates at the Port of Harwich which has daily sailings to Holland, another country which has several long distance walking routes. Old Harwich is a conservation area worthy of exploration before heading for home. Medieval in origin, it is a maze of narrow, interconnecting alleyways and is cared for by the Harwich Society. The Low and High Lighthouses are of particular interest, since at one time they were an important navigational aid in directing ships into the harbour.

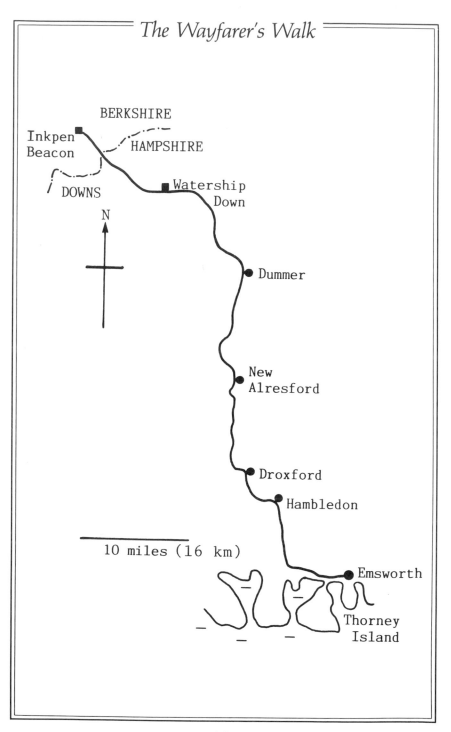

The Wayfarer's Walk

BERKSHIRE

Inkpen
Beacon

HAMPSHIRE

DOWNS

Watership
Down

N

Dummer

New
Alresford

Droxford

Hambledon

10 miles (16 km)

Emsworth

Thorney
Island

The Wayfarer's Walk

Information

Length	70 miles (113 km)
Start & finish	Emsworth (Grid ref. SU 755055)
	Inkpen Beacon (Grid ref. SU 365622)
Details of route	Emsworth – Warblington – Langstone Harbour – Bedhampton – Denmead – Forest of Bere – Hambledon – Droxford – Wind Farm – Kilmeston – Hinton Park – New Alresford – Abbotstone Down – Brown Candover – Dummer – Bull's Bushes – Oakley Park – Deane – The Portway – Watership Down – Ladle Hill – Seven Barrows – Highclere – Ashmansworth – Walbury Hill – Inkpen Beacon
Counties traversed	Hampshire. The last 1.5 miles (2.4 km) of the Way to Inkpen Beacon are in Berkshire
Nature of route	A Recreational or Regional LDP developed, funded and managed by Hampshire County Council. The route was created by linking together public footpaths, bridleways, green lanes and ancient trackways
Average duration	5–6 days
Landscape	Chalk ridges and downland. Ancient tracks. Farmland and villages
AONBs	The route starts in Chichester Harbour AONB, passes through East Hampshire AONB and finishes on the Hampshire/Berkshire border in the North Wessex AONB
Date of opening	The trail was opened and waymarked in 1981 and the first guidebook was produced in 1982
Waymarking	The route is waymarked with black WW symbols often accompanied by yellow or blue arrows. At intervals along the Way there are large wooden signposts indicating the distance from Emsworth and Inkpen Beacon
Navigation	Grade B
Maps	O.S. Landranger 1:50 000, Nos 197, 196, 185, 174
Linking LDPs	The Wayfarer's Walk links the Sussex Border Path at Emsworth with the Test Way at Inkpen Beacon
Shared LDPs	The first 3.5 miles (5.6 km) of the Wayfarer's Walk from Emsworth along Langstone Harbour to Langstone village is shared with the Solent Way.

The last 11 miles (17.7 km) from Watership Down to Inkpen Beacon are co-incident with the Inkpen Way (62 miles; 100 km, from Basingstoke to Salisbury)

Other LDPs
The Wayfarer's Walk crosses three other LDPs.
1 The SDW (Buriton to Winchester extension).
2 The South Wessex Way (117 miles; 188 km, from Petersfield to Poole Harbour).
3 King Alfred's Way (108 miles; 174 km, from Portsmouth to Oxford).
Note that further details of LDPs mentioned but not featured in this book can be found in the *Long Distance Walker's Handbook* by Barbara Blatchford & John Margetts (4th edition, 1990), published by A&C Black.

Transport
The start of the walk at Emsworth can be reached by British Rail. There are also stations at Warblington, Havant and Bedhampton. The nearest railway station to Inkpen Beacon is at Kintbury about 5 miles (8 km) away. Several bus routes cross or pass near to the line of the Wayfarer's Walk

Accommodation
There is a youth hostel at Overton, 2 miles (3.2 km) to the west of Deane. Details of other accommodation possibilities may be found in the guidebook

Guidebook
Wayfarer's Walk by Linda Herbst (2nd edition, 1989). Hampshire County Recreation. 96 pages. The sketch maps and drawings in this second edition are a great improvement on those in the first edition (published in 1982). The text contains much information on places of interest along the way. There is information about transport, accommodation and Tourist Information offices at the back of the book. It is available from Hampshire County Recreation Department (see Useful Addresses)

Shorter walks based on the Wayfarer's Walk
Hampshire Recreation Department also produce a number of leaflets describing shorter walks on or near to the route of the Wayfarer's Walk. These include three walks of between 2.75 miles (4.4 km) and 5.5 miles (8.9 km) around Abbotstone Down

Description

The Wayfarer's Walk was Hampshire's first LDP, created and maintained by the Recreation Department of the County Council. It is a

*Langstone Harbour, Hampshire. This tranquil area is traversed on both the
Solent Way and the Wayfarer's Walk*

complete south to north traverse of the eastern region of the county
from Emsworth on the West Sussex boundary to Inkpen Beacon on the
chalk downs just over the border in Berkshire. The path offers, as the
tourist blurb states, 'an invitation to explore Hampshire' in the best
possible way, that is on foot along an interconnecting series of footpaths, bridleways and green lanes. It provides a good selection of coastline, woodlands, rich green valleys and gentle rolling hills typical of the
county.

Much of Hampshire lies under chalk. Until modern times flint was the
major building material in the region and it is still seen on the walls of
many churches, cottages and old farm buildings. For centuries there was
plentiful trading in flint, salt and animals. The Wayfarer's Walk follows
several prehistoric and medieval tracks used by stone and iron age man
as trade routes and later by drovers, herding cattle to market. Three
ancient routes are crossed or incorporated into the Wayfarer's Walk, viz.
the North and South Hampshire Ridgeways and the Harrow Way. The
various tracks and paths of the Wayfarer's Walk cross modern farmland
(mainly arable and grassland for cattle) and traverse woodland to link up
a number of secluded and picturesque villages. The chalk pasture supports a rich flora, and skylarks and lapwing are common in the skies
above the chalk downland. The amateur naturalist and archaeologist are
well provided for on this cross-county path.

The first 3.5 miles (5.6 km) of the Wayfarer's Walk around Langstone

Harbour, with its abundant wintering wildfowl, are co-incident with the Solent Way. Soon after Langstone village the Wayfarer's Walk heads north to Bedhampton, where Keats finished his poem 'The Eve of St Agnes' and where in 1820 he spent his last night in England. From here the path climbs away from the clay and sand of the coastal strip on to a narrow chalk ridge, passing over Portsdown Hill towards Denmead and then on through an area once covered by thick woodland (the Forest of Bere) to Hambledon. Vines are now grown in this area, the dry white wine produced being bottled by Hambledon Vineyard.

The route heads towards the west for a time, leaving Hambledon with a stiff climb through Litheys Hanger, after which there is a stretch of fairly level walking before a descent into the Meon valley at Soberton. A riverside path is then followed north to Droxford. The Meon was fished by Izaak Walton (author of the fisherman's bible, *The Compleat Angler*) who considered it to be a fine trout river. Then follows the most wooded section of the walk through hazel, larch and beech woods to climb the valley of Betty Mundy's Bottom, named after an infamous legendary character. At the deserted medieval village of Lomer (an ancient monument) the Wayfarer's Walk joins the South Hampshire Ridgeway, a prehistoric track which ran from Kent to Salisbury Plain. Interestingly the best-known section of this track, the route along the chalk uplands of Sussex, has today become another long distance path, the South Downs Way. The South Hampshire Ridgeway is followed for about a mile (1.6 km) to Wind Farm, after which large open fields are crossed to the old village of Hinter Ampner nestling amongst lime and chestnut trees.

A medieval track leads to the charming village of Cheriton beside the River Itchen and from here the river is followed for a while, passing Tichborne Park before veering off to New Alresford. The River Itchen has associated watermeadows rich in wetland flora and there are several ancient tracks in the area. The region is steeped in legend and history; in particular an important defeat for the Royalists occurred at a battle near Cheriton during the Civil War in 1644.

New Alresford marks the half-way point on the Wayfarer's Walk. The town was once an important railway stop on the Mid-Hampshire 'Watercress Line' between Alton and Winchester. Alas the railway is today of little use to ramblers, although there is a private steam train operating between Ropley and New Alresford during summer weekends and holidays. From New Alresford the River Arle is followed for about a mile (1.6 km) before an ancient track climbs above the Upper Itchen valley and descends to the site of the medieval village of Abbotstone. Hampshire County Council now owns Abbotstone Down, fort. Despite its name there is no evidence that it was used during the Civil War.

The next section follows well-defined tracks over undulating downland and for a while the walk takes the Lunway, an ancient trade route between Old Sarum (near Salisbury) and Basingstoke. The Wayfarer's Walk passes close to Grange Park, site of The Grange, said to be one of Europe's outstanding neo-classical monuments. The way follows the Candover valley to Brown Candover before climbing again on quiet green lanes. Although only a few miles south of the M3 motorway, this an area of surprisingly remote, rolling downland. Between Becket's Down and Dummer the way passes an area dotted with several chalk pits. For many years mining for chalk was an important industry in the region, the chalk having a variety of uses from making lime paint and plaster to fertilising the soil. After crossing the M3 the path passes through Bull's Bushes Copse, a mixed woodland owned by the Forestry Commission, and crosses two railway lines either side of the village of Deane. The walk then meets the Harrow Way, one of the oldest prehistoric tracks in the country, probably in use 4000 years ago. It is part of the Pilgrims' Way from Kent and continued westwards to Salisbury Plain and on to Cornwall. In many places it has now become part of the modern road network.

The Wayfarer's Walk continues through the barley-growing area of North Hampshire to the Portway, the line of a Roman road which went from Salisbury to Silchester, south of Basingstoke. The remainder of the walk follows the North Hampshire Ridgeway, a prehistoric track following the high chalk ridge of the North Hampshire Downs. The North Hampshire Ridgeway can be walked from Basingstoke to the Vale of Pewsey where it joins the Great Ridgeway (see Ridgeway Path). Light aircraft in the skies above the downs (from a small airfield passed en route) and racing horses exercising on the gallops at White Hill are features of this section. The Way passes over Watership Down, home of the community of rabbits made famous by Richard Adams in the novel of the same name. Prehistoric man is in evidence on these chalk uplands in the form of barrows and hill forts. The iron age hill fort on Ladle Hill is passed en route. The disused Didcot, Newbury and Southampton Junction Railway is crossed before the trail climbs above the Highclere Estate, 6500 acres of finest-quality parkland and downland. The last few miles of the Wayfarer's Walk are in Berkshire. The route crosses Walbury Hill, at 974 ft (297 m) the 'county top' of Berkshire, and terminates at Combe Gibbet on the summit of Inkpen Beacon. There is a modern replica of the original gibbet that stood here for many years, a grim reminder of earlier times. The wide plain, 400 ft (122 m) below the escarpment, stretches far out to the north to the Lambourne Downs. The Beacon, lying on southern England's highest chalk downland, is a fitting end to a fine walk, but those wanting more can about turn and recross Hampshire on the Test Way (q.v.).

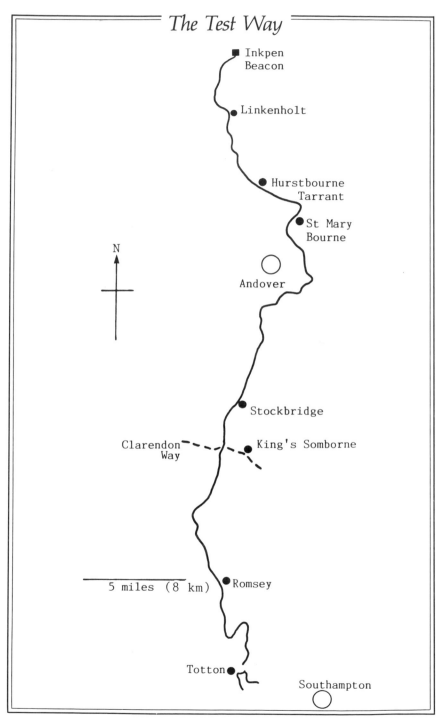

The Test Way

- Inkpen Beacon
- Linkenholt
- Hurstbourne Tarrant
- St Mary Bourne
- Andover
- Stockbridge
- Clarendon Way
- King's Somborne
- Romsey
- Totton
- Southampton

N

5 miles (8 km)

The Test Way

Information

Length	48 miles (77 km)
Start & finish	Totton, near Southampton (Grid ref. SU 360140) Inkpen Beacon (Grid ref. SU 365622)
Details of route	Totton – Romsey – Kimbridge – Mottisfont – Horsebridge – Stockbridge – Leckford – Chilbolton – Wherwell – Middleton – Harewood Forest – St Mary Bourne – Wallop Hill Down – Hurstbourne Tarrant – Linkenholt – Combe Wood – Inkpen Beacon
Counties traversed	Hampshire. The last couple of miles of the route follows the boundary between Berkshire and Wiltshire, the path terminating in Berkshire
Nature of route	A Recreational or Regional LDP developed, funded and managed by Hampshire County Council. Part of the route, along the disused Test Valley Railway, can be used by horseriders and cyclists
Average duration	3–4 days
Landscape	River valley, towns and villages. Woodland. Chalk escarpment
AONB	The final section of the walk is in the North Wessex Downs AONB
Date of opening	The route was waymarked in 1984. The first guidebook was published in 1986 although a leaflet providing essential details had appeared before that date
Waymarking	The route is waymarked with a green TW symbol on a white background
Navigation	Grade B
Maps	O.S. Landranger 1:50 000, Nos 196, 185, 174 O.S. Pathfinder 1:25 000, Nos SU: 21/31, 22/32, 23/33, 24/34, 44/54, 45/55, 25/35, 26/36
Alternative routes	By making use of the Clarendon Way (a 25-mile; 40.3 km LDP from Salisbury to Winchester which crosses the Test Way near King's Somborne, north of Horsebridge) the walker could start at Totton (or Inkpen Beacon) and walk to either Winchester or Salisbury. The Clarendon Way is described in the same guidebook (see below)
Other LDPs	The Test Way crosses the South Wessex Way at Romsey and meets with the Wayfarer's Walk on Inkpen Beacon

Transport	The start of the Way at Totton can be reached by British Rail and there is also a railway station at Romsey (0.6 mile; 1 km, off route). The nearest railway station to the end of the Test Way is at Kintbury about 5 miles (8 km) from Inkpen Beacon. Several bus services cross or pass near to the route (details in the guidebook)
Accommodation	Details of B & B, hotel and inn accommodation are given in the guidebook. Unfortunately there are no youth hostels on or near to the route but those walkers continuing on the Clarendon Way will find hostels at both Winchester and Salisbury
Guidebook	*Walks in Wessex. The Test Way and the Clarendon Way* by Barry Shurlock (1986), Hampshire County Council. 128 pages. The guidebook contains the relevant O.S. maps at 1:25 000 with the route overprinted. There is little route description but the text contains much detail of the architecture, history and natural history of the places passed en route. The book is illustrated with a selection of black and white photographs. The back of the work consists of an information section (public transport, car parks, where to stay, where to eat, places to visit). There is an extensive bibliography
Shorter walks based on the Test Way	See under Wayfarer's Walk

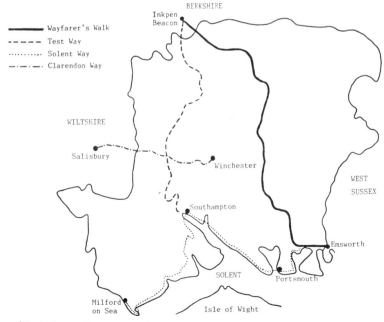

Hampshire's long distance paths

Description

The Test Way, like the Wayfarer's Walk, traverses the county of Hampshire from south to north. Both walks end at Inkpen Beacon on the chalk downs in Berkshire, but there the similarities end. The Test Way covers the western half of the county and for about two-thirds of its length, as its name suggests, follows the valley of the River Test. The path often borders the river itself, but at other times traverses the woods and fields above the valley bottom. The route starts at Totton where the River Test widens into an estuary which enters Southampton Water leading to the Solent. The river is followed upstream for approximately 27 miles (43.5 km) to Longparish where the Way and the Test part company. The river continues for about another 12 miles (19.3 km), bending to the north-east to Whitchurch and on to its source in the hills above Overton. The Test Way heads north for a further 20 miles (32.2 km) following the line of the River Bourne, a tributary of the Test, to the charming villages of St Mary Bourne and Hurstbourne Tarrant, before climbing the Downs to Inkpen Beacon.

The River Test is one of the great English rivers, renowned world wide for its game fishing, particularly trout. It is a wide chalk stream for much of its length with clear, sparkling waters which provide ideal sport for the fly fisherman. The river has attracted over the centuries some of the best and most influential anglers of the day and is the home of some of the most prestigious angling clubs in the land. The Test enters some of the finest countryside in southern England and a walk along its quiet waters will do much to refresh any jaded spirits brought on by the frantic pace of modern urban living.

The Test Way starts at the Salmon Leap pub on the outskirts of Totton and follows a line of footbridges across the marshland and reed beds of Ruddy Mead. This is a nature reserve managed by the Hampshire and Isle of Wight Naturalist's Trust and has been designated by the Nature Conservancy Council as a Site of Special Scientific Interest (SSSI). The brackish water supports a variety of rare plants and the site is the home of a number of birds and wintering wildfowl. The path passes under the M27 motorway and crosses over the west bank of the Test to Moorcourt. This area is a favourite of salmon fishermen.

The route heads north to the outskirts of Romsey. Across the river are the house and landscaped grounds of Broadlands, which was the home of Lord Louis Mountbatten. The house, dating from the 1770s, must rank as one of the finest stately homes in the country. It is open to the public. A detour into the town of Romsey is recommended for a visit to its fine abbey and other medieval buildings. Back on the Test Way the path enters Squabb Wood, deciduous woodland of oak, beech, silver birch and alder, and continues north to Mottisfont Abbey (National Trust) dating from the thirteenth century. These lower reaches of the

Test were constantly raided by the Danes in the tenth and eleventh centuries and the area abounds in tales of dark age atrocities. These are hard to imagine when faced with the peaceful scene of today.

Beneath the white cliffs of Lower Brook the Test Way meets and follows the disused Test Valley Railway for 10 miles (16.1 km) to Fullerton. The story of the railway, locally known as the Sprat and Winkle, is a familiar one. It was built in 1865, replacing the old canal that ran between Andover and Redbridge, but closed during the Beeching era in the 1960s. At Horsebridge, an important crossing point of the Test dating back to Roman times, the route passes the old station building, now a renovated private house, and continues to Stockbridge. This unspoilt market town, home of the prestigious Houghton Club, is best known for its fishing, although in years gone by it was a centre for horse racing.

The route takes the disused railway for much of the way between Stockbridge and Leckford, an unusual village in that it is entirely owned by the John Lewis Partnership who provide breaks for their staff at the nearby holiday camp. At Fullerton the Test Way leaves the railway track, which continued along the valley of the River Anton, to climb West Down from where there are fine views of the Test Valley. A descent leads to Chilbolton Common where a wooden footbridge crosses the Test to Wherwell. The route leaves the river for a couple of miles to take pleasant woodland paths through Harewood Forest.

At Longparish the Test Way departs from the main river and instead follows the line of the Bourne, a major tributary of the Test, passing well to the east of Andover and descending to the valley at St Mary Bourne. The path is now exploring some of the more remote parts of the county, little visited by the average tourist. St Mary Bourne is a delightful village nestling in a peaceful sylvan valley. Downstream near to the railway line is a large area of watercress beds which provide one of the main commercial interests in the valley. A succession of fields and small woods over Wallop Hill Down leads further upstream to the churchyard at Hurstbourne Tarrant. This village was the home of Joseph Blount, an eccentric and friend of William Cobbett, the author of *Rural Rides*, part of which was written in Blount's house in the village. Blount's enormous tombstone can be seen in the churchyard. Nearby Parsonage Farm has an interesting timber-framed granary on saddlestones. The Way passes close to the source of the Bourne Rivulet which dries up during most summers, but re-forms during the rains of the winter months.

After Ibthorpe a chalk and flint track leads over the rolling open downland of the upper Bourne valley, crossing the ancient earthwork of Grim's Ditch. The character of this last section of the walk is very different from the lush meadows of the Test Valley where the walk began. The path continues to Linkenholt, a small village in the heart of the 'Hampshire Highlands'. A sharp descent leads to a sheltered valley below Hart Hill Down which is followed into Combe Wood, an ancient oak wood. Hampshire is left for Berkshire which is soon exchanged for Wiltshire for a short while as the path climbs Sheepless Hill. The great chalk escarpment of the Downs provides a dramatic finale, the route making a sharp turn to the east to end at the gibbet on Inkpen Beacon.

The most recent LDP in Wessex in the Clarendon Way, a 25-mile (40.3 km) waymarked trail linking the great cathedral cities of Salisbury and Winchester. The walk takes its name from the medieval palace of Clarendon, the site of which it passes on the outskirts of Salisbury. The first third of the Way is in Wiltshire on a route from Salisbury to Pitton and Middle Winterslow. The path enters Hampshire, continuing to Broughton and crossing the Test Way near King's Somborne. Long stretches of open downland lead to Farley Mount Country Park on the outskirts of Winchester. Part of the route follows the line of the Roman road from Old Sarum to Winchester.

The Solent Way

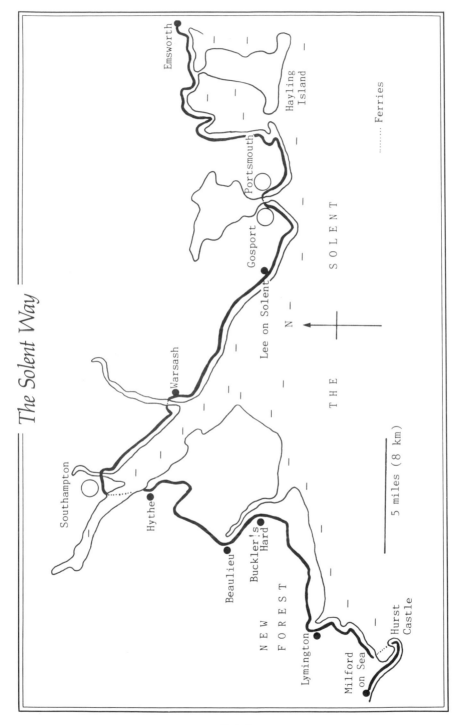

Emsworth

Hayling Island

Portsmouth

Gosport

.... Ferries

Lee on Solent

THE SOLENT

N

Warsash

Southampton

Hythe

Beaulieu

Buckler's Hard

NEW FOREST

Lymington

Milford on Sea

Hurst Castle

5 miles (8 km)

The Solent Way

Information

Length	60 miles (97 km)
Start & finish	Milford-on-Sea (Grid ref. SZ 292918)
	Emsworth (Grid ref. SU 755055)
Details of route	Milford-on-Sea – Hurst Castle – Keyhaven – Waterford – Lymington – Walhampton – Bucklers Hard – Beaulieu – Beaulieu Heath – Hythe – Southampton – Itchen Bridge – Woolston – Netley – Hamble – Warsash – Hill Head – Lee-on-the-Solent – Gosport – Portsea – Old Portsmouth – Southsea – Eastney – Langstone Harbour – Langstone – Emsworth
Counties traversed	Hampshire
Nature of route	A Recreational or Regional LDP established, funded and managed by Hampshire County Council
Average duration	4–5 days
Landscape	Coastline. Coastal marshes, mudflats, estuaries, beaches, heath, forest, castles, ships and museums. The route includes both urban and rural scenery
AONBs	The walk starts in Chichester Harbour AONB and later passes through the South Hampshire Coast AONB and the New Forest
Date of opening	1982. A guidebook was not published until 1984, but a leaflet on the route had appeared before then
Waymarking	The symbol of the Solent Way is a dark blue bird in flight on a light blue background. This appears at intervals along the Way
Navigation	Grade A
Maps	O.S. Landranger 1:50 000, Nos 195, 196, 197
	O.S. Pathfinder 1:25 000, Nos SU: 60/70, 40/50; SZ: 49/59, 29/39
	O.S. Outdoor Leisure Map 1:25 000 – New Forest
Linking LDPs	The Solent Way links both the Wayfarer's Walk and the Sussex Border Path at Emsworth with the Bournemouth Coast Path (20 miles; 32.2 km, from Sandbanks Ferry, Poole to Milford-on-Sea). The Solent Way, Bournemouth Coast Path and the South-West Way together constitute a continuous coastal footpath from Minehead in Somerset to

Emsworth on the Hampshire/West Sussex border, a distance of 640 miles (1 030 km)

Ferries

There are four ferries along the trail.
1 From Hurst Castle to Keyhaven. The ferry runs frequently (about every 30 mins) but only from Easter through the summer months. However, it is not essential to take this ferry in order to complete the walk. Instead the path out to Hurst Castle can be reversed and another path taken to Keyhaven.
2 Hythe to Southampton. Note that this ferry service does not operate on Sundays.
3 Hamble to the river bank north of Warsash. This service runs every day of the week throughout the year.
4 Gosport Hard to Portsea. There is a frequent foot passenger service.

Transport

The nearest British Rail station to the start of the walk is at New Milton, 4 miles (6.4 km) from Milford-on-Sea. The Solent Way finishes at Emsworth where there is a British Rail station. In between there are railway stations at Lymington Town, Southampton, Woolston, Netley, Portsmouth Harbour, Fratton, Bedhampton and Havant. There are several bus services along the route

Accommodation

There are youth hostels in Southampton and Portsmouth, and also at Burley in the New Forest (off route). There is plenty of hotel and guest house accommodation along the Way. Pubs, cafes and restaurants abound

Guidebook

The Solent Way. A Guide to Hampshire's Coast by Barry Shurlock (1984), Hampshire County Council. 130 pages. There is little route description but the book contains the relevant 1:25 000 O.S. maps with the Way marked in green. The text describes in detail the history and natural history of the places of interest passed en route. The rear of the book contains pages of information on public transport, where to park, where to stay, where to eat and places to visit. There is a selection of black and white photographs and a bibliography

Shorter walks based on the Solent Way

See under Wayfarer's Walk

Description

For those walkers with an interest in history, particularly naval history, and who have a penchant for visiting museums, there is little to beat the Solent Way LDP. There are probably more places of interest per mile of this path than along any other in the country. This, coupled with an abundance of public transport in the area, makes the route an ideal one for walking in short day or weekend stages, spending several hours of each day in one of the museums, castles or ships en route. By the time the walk has been completed the wayfarer should have a good appreciation of British maritime history from Tudor times to the present day.

The Solent Way was the second of the three LDPs to be developed by the forward-looking Hampshire County Council in the early 1980s. It is quite different in character from the other two, indeed from any other long distance path in the country, being predominantly a coastal footpath, part rural and part urban, the various sections of which are linked together by a number of ferry crossings. The trail is almost a complete traverse of Hampshire from Milford-on-Sea in the west (about 4.5 miles; 7.2 km, to the east of the county boundary with Dorset at High Cliff) to the eastern border with West Susex at Emsworth. On the way the route passes coastal marshes and river mouths, beaches and shingle spits, woods and fields, and visits numerous towns, villages and historic ports. The path follows the mainland to the north of the Solent and in so doing often presents fine views of the Isle of Wight. In addition a section of the New Forest, possibly the finest area of deciduous woodland remaining in the country, is included in the route of the Solent Way.

From the seafront of the pleasant holiday village of Milford-on-Sea there is a hard 2-mile (3.2 km) walk mainly on shingle beach along Hurst Castle Spit. From here a fine view of the Isle of Wight is obtained, the sea stacks of the Needles and the green hills of Tennyson Down being seen to good effect. Hurst Castle at the extremity of the promontory is the nearest point on the mainland to the Isle of Wight. Less than a mile separates Hurst Castle from Cliff End on the island. Binoculars may help to locate walkers on the Isle of Wight Coastal Footpath, a 65-mile (105 km) route which completely encircles the island. The ancient monument of Hurst Castle is open throughout the year. A ferry can be taken to Keyhaven Harbour to follow the sea wall around Keyhaven, Pennington and Oxney Marshes. These marshes, now a natural history reserve, were once an important industrial site used in the production of salt. Wildfowl are very numerous in the area, particularly during the autumn and winter months when redshank, dunlin, brent geese, grey plover and several other species migrate here from colder northern climes.

The Way passes marinas and large open-air swimming pools to reach the Royal Lymington Sailing Club. Yachting is the main activity in the region, the heart of Lymington being the area around the old quay. The route crosses Lymington River by a causeway, passes a granite obelisk on Mount Pleasant and continues through fields and along country lanes past Sowley Pond to Bucklers Hard. There is much to do here including a visit to the Maritime Museum and a short riverbus cruise on the Beaulieu River. Bucklers Hard was an important centre for ship building. The *Agamemnon*, Nelson's favourite ship, was launched from here in 1781. More recently it has associations with Sir Francis Chichester who single-handedly circumnavigated the world in 1966–7. A pleasant riverside walk of 2.5 miles (4 km) through woods and fields leads to Beaulieu village. The National Motor Museum is 2 miles (3.2 km) off route from here, but many will consider this to be an essential detour to visit the displays of vintage cars, the many exhibitions, abbey ruins and house. The Solent Way deviates inland for about 6 miles (9.7 km) to pass through woods to Hill Top and then across open Beaulieu Heath to Hythe on Southampton Water. From here a ferry crosses to Southampton.

There is much of interest in Southampton including the Maritime Museum, Tudor House Museum, Hall of Aviation and City Art Gallery. A pavement walk of 2 miles (3.2 km) leads down Canute Road and over Itchen Bridge, built in 1977, to Woolston. The path continues along the front of Southampton Water, past Netley and through the Royal Victoria Country Park. Here there is an exhibition on maritime Hampshire including a video film on the Solent Way. At Hamble a small but regular ferry takes the wayfarer across to Warsash. It was on the River Hamble that many of the landing craft used in the D-Day landings were assembled prior to sailing across the Channel. An unspoilt coastal path offering pleasant views across to Calshot and Cowes leads to Titchfield Haven, a nature reserve on the banks of the River Meon. The route continues to follow the beach over shingle and grassy open space, passing Hill Head and Lee-on-Solent to Gosport. The highlight here is an opportunity to go aboard a submarine at the Royal Navy Submarine Museum near Haslar Bridge.

The last ferry of the trip takes the walker across to Portsmouth. In the dockyards here there is enough to occupy a full day without leaving time for any walking at all. Portsmouth is the home of Nelson's flagship, HMS *Victory*, the *Mary Rose* exhibition and the Royal Naval Museum. A little further round the coast is Southsea where the exhibitions at the modern D-Day Museum in Southsea Castle are highly recommended. The museum was opened as part of the 40th anniversary of the D-Day landings. The castle houses displays on the maritime history and archaeology of the area. From Old Portsmouth the Solent Way continues along the sea front for 4 miles (6.4 km), passing yet another museum, that of the Royal Marines.

At Eastney the route turns to the north to join the Langstone Harbour sea wall path. Langstone Harbour, nearly 5000 acres of mudbanks and tidal water, is a haven for wildfowl. It is in sharp contrast to the developed areas of the Solent that have just been negotiated. Here all is tranquil and unspoilt. The sea wall is followed around the nature reserve for 10 miles (16.1 km), skirting the edge of Farlington Marshes to the village of Langstone. This old waterside village has a pleasant quay alongside the Royal Oak pub. The last few miles of the Solent Way cross fields facing Hayling Island to Warblington with its church and its castle remains, and finally to the old, small port of Emsworth, once famous for its oyster fleet. Although only 60 miles (96.6 km) in length, the Solent Way offers great variety and contrast of scenery with much to satisfy the inquisitive rambler.

Signpost at Emsworth, Hampshire

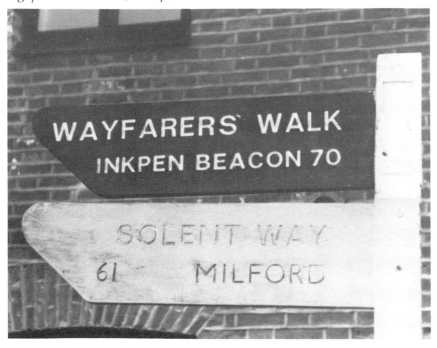

Useful Addresses

Ramblers' Association (RA), 1–5 Wandsworth Road, London SW8 2LJ. Tel. 071 582 6878.

Long Distance Walkers Association (LDWA), Membership Secretary, 7 Ford Drive, Yarnfield, Stone, Staffs ST15 0RP.

Youth Hostels Association (YHA), Trevelyan House, 8 St Stephen's Hill, St Albans, Herts AL1 2DY. Tel. 0727 55215.

Long Distance Paths Advisory Service (LDPAS), Administrator, The Barn, Holme Lyon, Burneside, Kendal, Cumbria LA9 6QX.

Countryside Commission, Publications, 19–23 Albert Road, Manchester M19 2EQ. Tel. 061 224 6287. A free 'Walking in Britain' poster-style leaflet detailing 59 LDPs throughout Britain is available from this address. Recommended.

Council for the Protection of Rural England (CPRE), Warwick House, 25 Buckingham Palace Road, London SW1W 0PP. Tel. 071 976 6433.

The Vanguards Rambling Club, c/o 109 Selsdon Park Road, South Croydon, Surrey CR2 8JJ.

Eastbourne Rambling Club, Secretary, 65 Westwood Avenue, Eastbourne, East Sussex BN22 0ES.

P & R Publicity (LDP achievement badges), Queensway, Stem Lane, New Milton, Hants BH25 5NN.

English Tourist Board, Thames Tower, Black's Road, Hammersmith, London W6 9EL. Tel. 071 730 3400.

South-East England Tourist Board, 1 Warwick Park, Tunbridge Wells, Kent TN2 5TA. Tel. 0892 40766.

Southern Tourist Board, 40 Chamberlayne Road, Eastleigh, Hants SO5 5JH. Tel. 0703 616027.

Thames & Chiltern Tourist Board, The Mount House, Witney, Oxfordshire, OX5 6DZ. Tel. 0993 778800.

Kent County Council, Land and Property, Springfield, Maidstone, Kent ME14 2LF. Tel. 0622 671411.

East Sussex County Council, Phoenix Causeway, Lewes, East Sussex BN7 1UE. Tel. 0273 478007.

West Sussex County Council, Planning Department, County Hall, Tower Street, Chichester, West Sussex PO19 1RL. Tel. 0243 777100.

Surrey County Council, Countryside Section, Planning Department, County Hall, Penrhyn, Kingston upon Thames KT1 2DT. Tel. 081 541 9453/9082 or 081 546 1050.

Hampshire County Recreation Department, North Hill Close, Andover Road, Winchester, Hants SO22 6AQ. Tel. 0962 846003.

Essex County Council, Planning Department, Globe House, New Street, Chelmsford CM1 1LF. Tel. 0245 352232.

Oxfordshire County Council, Ridgeway Officer, Department of Leisure and Arts, Central Library, Westgate, Oxford OX1 1DJ. Tel. 0865 810253.

British Rail Travel Enquiries, Tel. 071 928 5100 or 071 262 6767.

Romney, Hythe & Dymchurch Railway, New Romney Station, Kent TN28 8PL. Tel. 0679 62353.

Bus Companies. Telephone numbers for timetable enquiries:
Alder Valley 042873; Berks and Bucks 0494 20941; Brighton & Hove 0273 206666; Eastbourne Buses 0323 415900; East Kent 0843 581333; East Surrey 0342 893080; Essex bus information 0245 352232; Green Line 081 668 7261; Hants & Dorset 0962 52352; Lewes Coaches 0273 674881; London & Country 0737 242411; London Link 0734 794875; London Transport 071 222 1234; Maidstone & District 0892 26900; National Express 071 730 0202; Oxford Bus 0865 791579; RDH Services 0273 400711; Southdown 0273 474441 or 0323 27354; Thamesdown 0793 23700; Tillingbourne 0483 276880.

PERSONAL LOG OF THE LONG DISTANCE PATHS IN THE SOUTH-EAST

Ldp	Length miles km		Dates Start	Finish	Companions	Weather	Comments
South Downs Way	102	164					
North Downs Way	154	247					
Downs Link	30	48					
Wey South Path	36	58					
Greensand Way	105	169					
Wealdway	82	132					
Vanguard Way	62	100					
Sussex Border Path	150	242					

Mid-Sussex Link	37	60							
Saxon Shore Way	140	225							
South Coast Way	81	130							
London Countryway	205	330							
Ridgeway Path	85	137							
Thames Path	180	290							
Essex Way	81	130							
Wayfarer's Walk	70	113							
Test Way	48	77							
Solent Way	60	97							

Index